Foreword

Victor Mollo is arguably the best and surely the most amusing of all bridge writers. An old friend, he wrote the introduction to one of my books. Accordingly, I am delighted to write this foreword.

As a constant admirer of Victor's previous work, I was well prepared for an enjoyable experience. This is the other part of Mollo—the teacher rather than the humorist. The well-selected deals consistently produce a lesson.

What this book does so well is teach the reader how to think at the bridge table. Bridge is too complicated a game to play well simply by memorizing a set of rules. Learning certain principles is, of course, an excellent start. However, you cannot stop there. You must develop a sense of the reason for the rule, then face each problem for solutions within the framework of the basics. The learning process develops as you examine a series of problems and their solutions.

Placing the answers on the page following the problem is a fine technique. Searching for answers at some remote place in a book is often a bore; Mollo's setup makes it a pleasure.

His choice of problems is adroit. Solutions require strict attention to the evidence provided. That is the essence of scholarship at bridge. The reader learns that it takes time—and concentration on the options available—to find the correct answers. Some assumptions must be made: the conclusions then follow logically.

The major portion of these problems concentrates on slams, with a minimum of low-level contracts. Thus the gains or losses at stake are large. No matter what scoring system is in play—total points, IMPS, or match points—a whole session of rubber bridge, a match at team-of-four, or a session at match points—your final standing can be decided on one hand. Most deals are run-of-the-mill; the "big" hands have a major impact on a player's results.

Mollo has the rare gift of combining instruction with entertainment. In these pages, the teacher takes precedence over the humorist. The presentation of so many excellent problems and their available solutions will help the reader to succeed on important hands. Every reader will learn from and enjoy the lessons in this book. Mollo challenges and wins again! And so will you!

—Sam Stayman

Preface

I invite you to place your bet—after the race, of course. I will give you the winner now and challenge you to prove me wrong, later.

You are the winner I have marked on my card. You want to improve your bridge and I am prepared to guarantee that you will do so. Who is to decide? *You* will, acting both as judge and jury. What's more, you will have by your side a yardstick to measure your progress as you go along.

Your number will go up because you will not be able to help yourself as, willy-nilly, you imbibe the technique of winning, something which transcends the sum total of the manoeuvres and stratagems which make it up.

When will you know for certain that you have won? As soon as you have added up the scores for the first and the second hundred problems and compared the two. Inevitably, you will return a higher score on the second round and therein lies the crux of my challenge.

Do I detect a cynical smile? Can it be that you suspect me of hanky-panky, of stacking the pack against you by selecting easier problems for the second hundred than for the first? That could be done, of course, but since, like Caesar's wife, I must be above suspicion, I invite you, if you so desire, to start with problem 101. You will then return a higher score next time, for the first hundred. The order in which you answer the questions will make no difference, for though this is a play in two acts, neither precedes the other and Act II is as good a place to start as Act I, though no better. Hence my guarantee. Whichever way you do it, you can't avoid winning. Caesar's wife couldn't do that. What wife could?

The marriage between a text-book and instructional quizzes, of which we are about to see a happy consummation, allows the reader to make the best of both worlds, to win on the swings and on the round-abouts, which is, you will agree, the essence of fair play.

But now I have a confession to make. I have plagiarised—myself. I introduced the concept of a challenge, with a built-in yardstick, some years ago, first in a book on dummy play, now out of print, then in *The Case for the Defence,* which is very much in being. The idea was quickly crowned with success, so I have perfected and enlarged upon it, and now present what would be described in computer parlance as a new generation challenge.

The case for a happy marriage needs no elaboration. For the uninitiated a text-book is much the best medium for imparting information. The mechanics of every manoeuvre can be set out, explained in detail and copiously illustrated. But with no chapter headings to guide him at the bridge table, how will the student know which play is right for the occasion? This is where the quiz comes into its own. Pitched at the more experienced performer, with no helpful clues in its presentation, it puts the emphasis on identification. The diagnosis precedes the cure. Is a safety play required to insure against bad breaks? Are we short of a winner and must look to a squeeze or end-play for the extra trick? Or is there a loser to spirit away before defenders can get at it? Is a suit blocked? Do we lack entries? Have we too many trumps or too few? Two hundred times in these pages the reader will face such problems, with no continuity, no sub-titles, as in a text-book, to point the way. Disorder has been carefully planned at every stage. Different themes intermingle. Some of the easier problems coast side by side with those that are more difficult. The reader must do all the work himself, recognise the nature of the problem and solve it, before turning over-leaf for the answers.

There are marks to lose as well as to earn. The penalties are for mistakes due to carelessness, for 'doing what comes naturally' without thinking of the consequences, a deadly habit and a costly one, whether you play for money, matchpoints or IMPs.

On a rough and ready basis I have awarded five points for the easier problems, ten for those that are more difficult. The dividing line is often blurred and I have doubtless erred here and there, underestimating the complexity of some problems, overrating the simplicity of others. Fortunately I had room to spare. The winner I have promised you will not flash past the post in a photo-finish. He will be lengths ahead, so I can well afford the occasional lapse, knowing that you will easily make up for my shortcomings.

Act I

Curtain Raiser

There's nothing up my sleeve, no traps for the unwary, and above all, no abstruse conventions in the bidding to obscure the clarity of the play. Most of the time the auction will have no part in the proceedings. Occasionally, when it holds clues to the distribution or helps declarer to place the high cards, it will be recorded. Not otherwise. Our 1NT is always of the weak 12-14 species. There's little to choose between one type and another, but much to be said for adhering to the same range throughout.

Percentages, statistics, probabilities, come into our lives only when they really matter. *De minimis non curat lex* and neither do we. There's scope on every hand for elementary arithmetic. For higher mathematics there's none, which is why a computer is no more likely to play good bridge than to write an ode to a Grecian Urn or to paint a Mona Lisa. Happily, bridge is an art, not a science.

You will learn more from the answers that elude you than from those that come too easily, but all the problems should put you on your mettle and stimulate the little grey cells, for as in travel, so in bridge, the journey is more important than the arrival.

1

♠ 10 6		♠ 8 5 4
♡ A K Q J 10 9 7		♡ 8
◇ Q J 8		◇ A 10 7 6 5
♣ 7		♣ K Q 10 9

After three passes, West opened 4♡ and all passed. North led out the ♠AKQ. West ruffed, drew trumps and went down, and complained that everything was wrong. 'Including the play,' murmured East.

Where did West go wrong and which E/W cards should have made up the decisive trick?

2

♠ A 5 2		♠ 8 7 4
♡ A K 3 2	N W E S	♡ Q
◇ 8 6 3		◇ A 7 5 2
♣ A 6 5		♣ K J 4 3 2

North leads the ◇K, then the ◇Q against 3NT, South following. The ◇A goes up.

Which E/W cards should make up the next (third) trick?

3

♠ 7 6 3		♠ A K 10 2
♡ K 4	N W E S	♡ Q 10 3
◇ A K J 6 5		◇ 10 9 2
♣ Q J 10		♣ A K 9

Contract 3NT. Looking for partner's suit, North leads the ♡9 and finds it. South encourages with the ♡7 and West wins.

Which E/W cards should make up the next trick?

---

1 Trick four; ♣ 7 — ♣ 9   Marks: 10

Having passed originally, North, who produced the ♠AKQ, couldn't have the ♣A and was unlikely to have the ◇K. So, after ruffing the third spade high, West finesses the ♣9, losing maybe to the ♣J.

Whatever the return (a trump is best), West is in dummy with the ♡8 to take a ruffing finesse against the ♣A, setting up two clubs for diamond discards.

2 ♣ 2 — ♣ 5   Marks: 5

If the clubs are 3-2 the contract is unbreakable and if South has four it is unmakeable. What if North has four? By giving up a club West still scores the four he needs — if he can get to dummy. The ♡Q? Then, since the ♣A will surely be knocked out, how will he get back to the ♡AK? The answer is to lose the *first* club, retaining the ♣A as an entry. The marked finesse will follow. Alternatively, if West cashes the ♡Q and continues with the ♣A, he must duck the next club, even if North produces the ♣Q.

3 ♠ 3 — ♠ 10   Marks: 5

If the diamonds can be brought in safely all will be well, but losing the lead to North might be fatal, so West should give himself the extra chance of a 3-3 spade break. If it doesn't materialise, there'll still be time to test the diamonds, the ◇A, then the ◇K, in case of a doubleton ◇Q with North.

Meanwhile, South cannot lead a heart profitably, which is all that matters.

4

♠ A Q J		♠ 5 4
♡ A Q 2	N	♡ 6 3
◊ Q J 9 6 2	W E	◊ A 10 8 4 3
♣ A J 3	S	♣ 10 7 6 2

North leads the ♡7 against 3NT. South plays the ♡J and West wins.
Which E/W cards should make up trick two?

5

♠ K Q J 10 6 2		♠ 9 8 4
♡ 4	N	♡ A Q 7
◊ J 8 7	W E	◊ K Q 6 5
♣ J 10 6	S	♣ K Q 5

North leads the ♣9 against 4♠. South wins with the ♣A and returns the
◊10. West goes up with the ◊J on which North plays the ◊9.
Which E/W cards should make up the next trick?

6

♠ A K J 10		♠ 6 5 3 2
♡ A J 9 7	N	♡ 8 5
◊ 6 3	W E	◊ A K Q J 10
♣ J 5 2	S	♣ 10 6

North leads out the ♣AKQ against 4♠. Ruffing in dummy, West finesses
the ♠J which holds.
Which E/W cards should make up the next trick?

---

4   ♠ Q — ♠ 4   Marks: 10

West needs a second spade for his contract and he must set it up first, since the ♠K could be a vital entry to North's hearts. After holding up the ♡A it will be safe to finesse in diamonds. If South has the ◇K and a fourth heart, the suit won't be dangerous. The ♠A before the ♠Q? That could be fatal if South had both the ♠K and the ◇K.

---

5   ♡ 4 — ♡ Q   Marks: 10

The tocsin has sounded. South has a doubleton diamond, and as soon as the defence gains the lead with the ♠A, he will get a ruff. West's only hope is to discard a diamond before giving up the lead. If the heart finesse fails, he will go two down, but that's well worth the risk.

---

6   ♠ 10 — ♠ 5   Marks: 5

The pleasant road to ruin is to cross in diamonds and repeat the trump finesse. Yes, but what if North, with ♠Qxxx, was holding up the ♠Q? He can't be kept out and another diamond from him, while he retains a trump, will kill the suit.

The ♠10, after the ♠J, will allow *all* the trumps to be drawn. Meanwhile one trump remains in dummy to stop the clubs.

7
    ♠ J 10 9 3   ♠ Q 8 6 5
    ♡ J 10   N   ♡ A Q
    ◇ K 6 3   W E   ◇ A 4 2
    ♣ A K Q 2   S   ♣ J 10 4 3

Contract 4♠.

North leads the ♠K, ♠A and ♠4. At trick three South throws a nondescript heart.

Which E/W cards should make up the next trick? If it's a winner, the one after?

8
    ♠ Q J 2   ♠ A 10 6
    ♡ 7 5   N   ♡ A J 10 2
    ◇ A J 10 9 8 7   W E   ◇ K
    ♣ 8 6   S   ♣ A J 10 4 2

North leads the ♠4 against 3NT. Whichever way he plays West will win the first trick.

Which E/W cards should make up the next one?

9
    ♠ A   ♠ 10 8 6 5 2
    ♡ Q J 10 9 8 7   N   ♡ K 6
    ◇ A K Q 4 2   W E   ◇ 7 3
    ♣ A   S   ♣ J 9 7 3

North leads the ♠K against 6♡. West starts with the ◇AK and ruffs a diamond, South throwing a spade.

Which E/W cards should make up the next trick?

---

7 $\diamond$ 3 — $\diamond$ A; $\diamond$ 2 — $\diamond$ K   Marks: 10

The heart finesse won't run away. Meanwhile West can give himself an extra chance. After eliminating the clubs, three rounds of diamonds may leave South on play. If so, he will have to lead a heart or concede a ruff and discard. But, of course, once the clubs are played off he will see what's coming and promptly jettison his high diamonds. So as not to arouse South's suspicions the $\diamond$A and $\diamond$K should be played at once.

8 $\diamond$ K — $\diamond$ A (*not* $\diamond$ A — $\diamond$ K)   Marks: 5

West must go up at once with the ♠A. If he doesn't and North has the ♠K — or South, with ♠Kxx, plays low — he will surely go down. Keeping ♠QJ as a certain entry West overtakes the $\diamond$K and drives out the $\diamond$Q. No return from South can hurt. On a heart or club from North, West will insert dummy's 10. Whatever the return, he will come back with a spade to score four more diamonds.

9   ♣ 3 — ♣ A or ♠ 2 — ♡ 7   Marks: 10
         ♡ K — ♡ 7   Marks: -5

The only danger is that coming in with the ♡A North will lead his fourth diamond, which South will ruff. West must, therefore, remove North's last diamond before letting him in with the ♡A — if he has it. 'Doing what comes naturally' many a West would lead a trump. That's a thoughtless play and incurs a penalty.

10

    ♠ K 2   ♠ 8 7 6 5 3
    ♡ K J 9 8 7 6   ♡ A Q 10
    ♢ A K 7   ♢ 6 3 2
    ♣ Q 10   ♣ A 9

North leads the ♢Q against 4♡.

    Which E/W cards should make up trick two?

11

    ♠ 8 4 2   ♠ A Q 9
    ♡ J 5 3   ♡ 8 7 2
    ♢ A K 5   ♢ Q 9 3 2
    ♣ J 10 5 4   ♣ A K Q

Contract 3NT. Defenders lead hearts and take the first four tricks, then switch to a club. Two more clubs follow.

    Which E/W cards should make up the next trick?

12

    ♠ 10   ♠ A 5 4 3 2
    ♡ K Q 10 8   ♡ A J 9
    ♢ K Q J 10   ♢ A 2
    ♣ K J 9 4   ♣ 8 5 3

North leads the ♠K against 4♡.

    Which ten tricks does West expect to make?

10   ♠ 2 — ♠ 3   Marks: 5

Allowing for the likely 4-2 break West has the entries to set up a long spade for his tenth trick, but only if he starts at once. Should he take a round of trumps first, and find them 3-1, defenders will lead trumps each time they come in, leaving dummy short of an entry. There's nothing to gain by leading the ♠K and just the chance that the ♠A could be bare.

11   ◇ Q — ◇ 5   Marks: 5

West looks to the spade finesse or a 3-3 diamond break for his ninth trick. Which should it be? The finesse is a 50-50 chance while the odds against the 3-3 split are roughly 2-1. There's no reason, however, why West shouldn't eat his cake and have it, too. He takes three rounds of diamonds first, ending in his hand. Now he knows whether or not he requires the spade finesse.

12   ♠ A; four spade ruffs; ◇ K, ◇ A, two
           diamond ruffs; ♡ A   Marks: 10

If he draws trumps West has only nine tricks, so he embarks on a cross-ruff. The sequence is: ♠A, spade ruff; ◇K, ◇A, spade ruff. Two master diamonds are now ruffed to provide entries for two more spade ruffs.

13.   ♠ 7   ♠ A Q J 4 2
       ♡ A Q 9 7 6 5 3   ♡ J 10 8 4
       ◇ A K J   ◇ 10 6
       ♣ A Q   ♣ J 2

North leads the ♠5 against 6♡. Going up with dummy's ♠A West leads the ♡J, South following with the ♡2.
   Which card should West play?

14   ♠ 4   ♠ A 7 3 2
      ♡ Q 10 9 7 4   ♡ 8 6 5 3 2
      ◇ A K 10 8   ◇ 6 3
      ♣ K 9 4   ♣ A 8

North leads the ♠Q against 4♡. West goes up with dummy's ♠A.
   Which E/W cards should make up trick two?

15   ♠ K 9 7 4 3   ♠ A 8 6 5 2
      ♡ K 4 2   ♡ A J 3
      ◇ K 6 3   ◇ A 7
      ♣ K 2   ♣ A 9 4

North leads the ♣Q against 6♠. West wins and lays down the ♠A on which North throws a diamond.
   Assuming that he retains the lead until then, which will be the last five cards in the E/W hands?

---

13   ♡3   Marks: 5

By itself the finesse is roughly an even-money chance (52 to 48 against it). Here it's a 100 per cent certainty, for if it fails, whatever North returns will yield West his twelfth trick. If it's a diamond, a club will be discarded from dummy on the third round.

A spade will set up a trick whoever has the ♠K.

---

14   *Not* hearts   Marks: 0
          Hearts   Marks: -5

When this hand came up in a match, West, obeying some primeval instinct, played a trump. South showed out and North promptly cashed his ♡AKJ, leaving West with two trumps in each hand to look after three losers in the other. So long as declarer doesn't touch trumps he cannot go down. He will still lose tricks to the ♡AKJ, of course, but he will score ten himself.

---

15   W: ♠ 9 7 ♡ K 4 2 – E: ♠ 8 6 ♡ A J 3   Marks 5

Leaving South with the master trump, West will cash the ♣AK and the ◇AK, then ruff a club in his hand and a diamond in dummy. Having eliminated the minors, he will throw South in with a trump, forcing him to lead into dummy's heart tenace or to concede a ruff and discard.

The hand illustrates the basic mechanics of the elimination end-play. Other examples will be harder, some much harder.

---

16 ♠ A K Q 6   ♠ 7 5
        ♡ 10 6   N   ♡ J 3
        ◇ 10 9 3 W   E   ◇ A Q J 8 6 2
        ♣ A K 6 4   S   ♣ 8 5 3

North leads the ♡K and ♡A against 4♠, then switches to a club.
  Which E/W cards should make up trick four?

---

17 ♠ K 4 3   ♠ 7 5
        ♡ 2   N   ♡ A K 6
        ◇ 5 3 2   W   E   ◇ A 10 8 7 6
        ♣ A K J 8 7 6 S   ♣ Q 10 9

North, who called 1♠ over West's 1♣, led the ♡Q against 5♣. Though
South had the ◇KJ9 and North the ♠AQ, West made his contract.
  Which two tricks did he lose?

---

18 ♠ K Q 10 9 7 3   ♠ A 8
        ♡ A 6 3   N   ♡ 8
        ◇ A K Q   W   E   ◇ 7 6 4
        ♣ Q   S   ♣ A 8 6 5 4 3 2

West	North	East	South
2♠	4♡	6♠	Pass
Pass	Pass		

North led the ♡K, South following. Allowing for the not unlikely 4-1
trump break, West took no chances and proceeded to make his contract.
  Which E/W cards made up trick two?

---

16   ♠ 6 — ♠ 5   Marks: 5

Unless the diamond finesse succeeds and trumps break reasonably, there's no hope. But one defender must have four trumps, and if declarer takes his three top trumps first, the third diamond will be ruffed, cutting him off from dummy. Giving up the first trump will allow West to draw *four* rounds, removing the last one before turning to the diamonds. Meanwhile a trump remains in dummy, so he can't be forced.

---

17   ♡ Q (trick one); ♠ A   Marks: 5

The key play was to duck the ♡Q, discarding two diamonds later on the ♡AK. Using trumps as entries two long diamonds were then set up without letting in South. Unkindly, West pointed out that a trump switch at trick two would have removed a vital entry prematurely. North drew West's attention to the nine cold tricks available in 3NT. Jeers were even, but West scored the points.

---

18   ♡ 3 — ♠ A   Marks: 5

If, as was likely enough, South's heart was a singleton, and he had the ♠J, he would over-ruff dummy's ♠8 and return a trump, leaving West with a losing heart. Hence the high ruff at trick two. After that the over-ruff couldn't hurt for West could afford to lose a trump, so long as he didn't lose a heart as well.

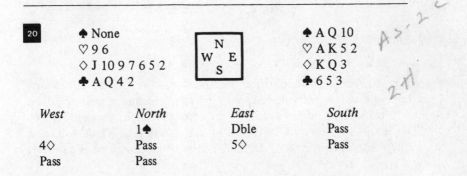

19
♠ A 10 5 3 2
♡ 10
◇ K Q J 8
♣ K 5 2

♠ 9
♡ A Q 8 5 4
◇ A 10 9 7
♣ A 6 4

North, who opened the bidding with 1♡, leads the ♣Q against 6◇. West wins in dummy.

Which E/W cards should make up trick two?

20
♠ None
♡ 9 6
◇ J 10 9 7 6 5 2
♣ A Q 4 2

♠ A Q 10
♡ A K 5 2
◇ K Q 3
♣ 6 5 3

West	North	East	South
	1♠	Dble	Pass
4◇	Pass	5◇	Pass
Pass	Pass		

North led the ◇A, South following, and switched to the ♡J. Regretting that he wasn't in 3NT, West needed a little luck, found it and went on to make his contract.

(a) Which E/W cards made up the next two tricks?
(b) Which trick, apart from the ◇A, did West lose?

21
♠ 8 2
♡ A K 5
◇ 6 5 3
♣ 10 9 8 7 6

♠ A K 9
♡ J 8 3
◇ A 7 4 2
♣ K Q 2

North led the ♡2 against 3NT. South covered dummy's ♡J with the ♡Q, held the trick and returned another heart. On a club (trick three) North went up with the ♣A. The story had a happy ending.

Which was the key play?

---

19   ♣ 4 — ♣ K   Marks: 5
        Trumps   Marks: −5

The heart finesse is doubtless right, but it's a mirage for West has twelve certain tricks on a complete cross-ruff, without finessing anything. But he must be careful not to lose the ♣K. While he cross-ruffs the majors, defenders will discard clubs, then ruff the ♣K. As always in a cross-ruff, side-suit winners should be cashed first.

---

20   (a) ♡ K — ♡ 9; ♡ 2 — ◊ 6   Marks: 5
        (b) ♠ 10 — ♣ 2   Marks: 5

A partial elimination was West's best chance, so he ruffed a third heart, hoping that North would have no more, and crossing in trumps led the ♠10 on which he threw a club. If, as he hoped, North, who had bid 1♠, had the ♠KJ, he would be forced to lead a club into West's ♣AQ or a spade into dummy's ♠AQ. Dummy's third trump remained as an entry.

---

21   ♣ K (Q) under ♣ A   Marks: 5

That North would play a third heart, killing West's only entry, was a cold-stone certainty. The only hope was to drop the ♣J, not so remote on North's play of the ♣A. So West unblocked and fortune smiled. North had started with ♣AJ bare. This is the moral: when the sun is out, be a pessimist, look for snags. When the clouds gather, be an optimist. Let wishful thinking be the order of the day.

22

♠ 2		♠ A J 9
♡ A Q 2		♡ 10 8 4
◇ A K 10		◇ Q 5 3
♣ A K Q J 10 8		♣ 9 7 6 5

North leads the ♠K against 6♣. West goes up with dummy's ♠A.
Which E/W cards should make up trick two?

23

♠ A 10 4		♠ K Q 6 5
♡ Q 10 7 6		♡ 3
◇ J 6 5 4		◇ A
♣ A 10		♣ K Q 9 8 6 4 2

North leads the ♠2 against 3NT.
Which E/W cards should make up trick two?

24

♠ A 10 6		♠ J 7
♡ J 7		♡ A Q 5 4 2
◇ Q 8 6		◇ A 7 5 4
♣ K J 10 9 8		♣ Q 4

West	*North*	*East*	*South*
	1♠	Pass	Pass
2♣	Pass	2♠	Pass
2NT	Pass	3♡	Pass
3NT	Pass	Pass	Pass

North leads the ♠5.
Which is the key play, likely to decide the fate of the contract?

---

22   ♠9 − ♣10   Marks: 10

That is the key play. After drawing trumps West will cash the ◇AK, cross to the ◇Q and lead the ♠J, throwing his ♡2, a *loser-on-loser* play. Spades and diamonds having been eliminated, North will be forced to lead a heart into the ♡AQ or to concede a ruff and discard.

---

23   ♣2 − ♣10   Marks: 10

West would like to be in 6♣. He isn't, so the problem is: what can go wrong in 3NT? If South has ♠Jxxx he might also have ♡A9x or ♡K9x, and if so, the 9 would allow defenders to take four heart tricks. So West gives up the free finesse in spades, which he doesn't need, to insure against an unlucky club break. A heart from North would not allow defenders to score more than three heart tricks, whatever the distribution.

---

24   ♠ J at trick one   Marks: 5

If North has ♠KQ the play at trick one won't matter. Should South have an honour, playing low from dummy will ensure two stoppers, but what of the other seven tricks? Winning the second club, North will lock declarer in dummy with the ♠J and there will be no way back. If South has a spade honour North must surely have both the red kings.

After unblocking in spades at trick one West can hardly fail to come to nine tricks.

---

25   ♠ K Q   ♠ A 10 5

       ♡ Q   N   ♡ 5 4 3

       ◇ K Q J 10 6 5   W   E   ◇ 9 8 7

       ♣ A J 7 2   S   ♣ K Q 10 9

North leads the ♣3 against 5◇.

    Which E/W cards should make up the next three tricks?

26   ♠ 5 3 2   ♠ A 7 4

       ♡ A Q 9 7 6 4   N   ♡ J 5 3 2

       ◇ J 9 4   W   E   ◇ A Q 10 2

       ♣ 6   S   ♣ Q J

West is in the somewhat optimistic contract of 4♡. North leads the ♠K to dummy's ♠A.

    Which card should be led from dummy at trick two?

27   ♠ A Q 4 3   ♠ 6 5

       ♡ 10 9 8 7 6 5 2   N   ♡ A K 3

       ◇ None   W   E   ◇ 10 4

       ♣ K Q   S   ♣ A 7 6 5 4 2

After a 3◇ opening by North, E/W, refusing to be intimidated, reach 6♡. North leads the ◇K which West ruffs.

    Which E/W cards should make up the next two tricks?

25 ♠ K – ♠ 5; ♠ Q – ♠ A; ♠ 10 – ♡ Q   Marks: 10

The ♣3 looks every pip a singleton, so a club ruff threatens. If South
has the ◇A Nemesis will win, but if the aces are divided and South's
share is the ♡A, West can cheat fate. On the ♠10 at trick four he
jettisons his ♡Q, unless South covers. Now, when North comes in with
the ◇A, he can no longer put South in, communications having been
cut by the *Scissors Coup.*

26   ♡ J   Marks: 0
          ♡ 2   Marks: –5

If trumps break 2-1 it is immaterial which card is led from dummy, but
should they be divided 3-0 only the lead of the ♡J will allow a second
finesse against South's ♡10.

27   ♣ K – ♣ 2; ♣ Q – ♣ 4   Marks: 10

West exposes himself deliberately to the danger of a ruff. Say that
either defender ruffs the ♣Q. West will win the next trick and cash
the ♡AK, leaving no trump out. A club ruff will now provide three
discards — ♣A76 — for the spades with the ♡3 as an entry, West having
carefully preserved the ♡2, of course. The contract will be made
despite a 4-1 break in clubs and 3-0 in trumps.

28

♠ Q
♡ 9 8
◇ K 6 4 3 2
♣ 8 7 5 3 2

♠ A 7 5 4
♡ A K 6 5
◇ A Q J
♣ A K

Having responded 2◇ to 2♣ West becomes declarer in 6◇. North leads the ♡2 to dummy's ♡K.

Which twelve tricks does West expect to score?

29

♠ 4 3
♡ A Q 9 8 7 6
◇ K 10 4
♣ A 4

♠ A K 2
♡ 5 4 3
◇ A J 6 5 3
♣ 3 2

North leads the ♣Q against West's 4♡. Declarer wins.

Which E/W cards should make up the next two tricks?

30

♠ 10 9
♡ A K 2
◇ A Q
♣ A K J 10 9 8

♠ A Q 7
♡ 10 9 3
◇ 10 9 3 2
♣ Q 3 2

North leads the ♣6 against 5♣. Both defenders follow to a second round of trumps. Having missed 3NT, exploring slam prospects, West can't take chances now.

Which E/W cards should make up the next (third) trick?

28   Dummy's eight top cards and four ruffs
         in the closed hand   Marks: 10

The quality of dummy's trumps and the number of entries in dummy point to a *dummy reversal*. West ruffs one heart and three spades, the last one with the ◊K. Dummy remains with ♡6 ◊QJ (the ◊A was the first re-entry) and the ♣K. So long as the ♣K isn't ruffed West has twelve tricks. The mechanism of the dummy-reversal consists in using the long trumps, usually in declarer's hand, to ruff losers, and the short trumps, usually in dummy, as here, to draw trumps.

29   ♡ A − ♡ 3; ♠ 4 − ♠ K   Marks: 10

West will cash the ♠A, ruff the ♠2 and exit with a club. A third club or diamond return by either defender will dispose of the possible diamond loser. A trump will ensure that there will be only one trump loser. Ten tricks whatever happens.

30   ◊ A − ◊ 2   Marks: 10

Followed by the ◊Q. If North wins and returns a spade (best) West will rise with dummy's ace and lead the ◊10, discarding a spade. The ◊9 will now take care of the losing heart.

31
♠ 6 5 4   ♠ A 3 2
♡ A 7 5   ♡ Q J
◇ A K 4 2   ◇ J 10
♣ A K Q   ♣ J 10 8 7 5 3

```
      N
   W     E
      S
```

North leads the ♠Q against 3NT, low from dummy and the ♠K from South, who returns the ♠7.

How many tricks should West make if
(a) North has the ♡K and ◇Qxx?
(b) South has those cards?

32
♠ 10 9 8   ♠ J 5
♡ K Q J 9 8 7   ♡ A 10 6
◇ J 10   ◇ A 8 5 2
♣ K J   ♣ A 5 4 3

```
      N
   W     E
      S
```

North leads the ◇3 against 4♡. West rises with dummy's ◇A.
Which E/W cards should make up trick two?

33
♠ K J 10 7 6   ♠ A Q 9 8
♡ A   ♡ 10 5 2
◇ A J 8 2   ◇ 10 5 4
♣ 8 5 4   ♣ A K 2

```
      N
   W     E
      S
```

South, dealer, bids 1◇. Undeterred, E/W sail into 6♠. North leads a low heart. Crossing twice in trumps West ruffs two hearts, defenders following all the way in both suits.

Which E/W cards should make up the next two tricks?

31   (a) and (b) Nine   Marks: 10

West mustn't hold up the ♠A a second time. If South has a third spade — very unlikely on his return of the ♠7 — the suit isn't dangerous. But there's another reason. After cashing the ♣AKQ, West will throw North in with a spade. Having taken two more spades he will have to lead a red card. It will present West with a trick in that suit and give access to dummy's remaining club. Two will have to be thrown on North's spades.

32   Spades   Marks: 5
        A trump   Marks: –5

West's tenth trick will be a spade ruff, so he mustn't give defenders the chance to lead trumps three times. 'Just' one round of trumps could be fatal.

33   ♣A – ♣4; ♣K – ♣5   Marks: 10

North clearly has no diamond, so South has six. Having followed to five cards in the majors he cannot have more than two clubs. West removes them and leads dummy's ◇4, covering South's card — the ◇7 with the ◇8, the ◇Q with the ◇A. Next he leads the ◇2 to dummy's ◇10. South wins, but having no safe exit, must return another diamond into West's tenace. Dummy's club loser disappears on West's fourth diamond.

34

♠ A K Q J 8 5		♠ 10 6 2
♡ 10 7 4	**N**	♡ K 8
◇ 7 3 2	**W E**	◇ A K 8 5 4
♣ 5	**S**	♣ K 8 4

In response to a strong 3♣ overcall by South over East's 1◇, North leads the ♣9 against 4♠. South takes the ♣K with the ♣A and continues with the ♣Q. Trumps break 2-2.

Which three tricks should West lose?

35

♠ A 8 6 5 4 2		♠ K Q
♡ A 3	**N**	♡ J 10 2
◇ K J	**W E**	◇ A 7 6 5 4 3
♣ A J 4	**S**	♣ 8 3

North leads the ♣K against 3NT, holds the trick and switches to a spade.

Which E/W cards should make up the third and fourth tricks?

36

♠ A Q 9		♠ K J 10
♡ A K Q 8	**N**	♡ J 10 9
◇ A Q 4	**W E**	◇ J 6 5 2
♣ A J 3	**S**	♣ K 6 5

North leads a spade against 6NT. West wins in dummy and finesses the ◇Q which holds.

Which E/W cards should make up the next trick?

34   *Two* clubs; one heart   Marks: 10

After drawing trumps West crosses to the ◇A and leads the ♣8 discarding a diamond. South returns a diamond, but West ruffs a third diamond, setting up two winners for heart discards. The opening lead of the ♣9 guaranteed that the ♣8 couldn't be won by North. Rising with the ♣K at trick one was an essential part of the strategem.

This is how the hand was played in a top-class tournament by the American international, Norman Kay.

35   ◇ 3 – ◇ K; ◇ J – ◇ A   Marks: 10

West has seven top tricks. Only spades or diamonds can provide two more, and either suit may break badly, but unless both do all should be well. West tests each suit in turn. If all follow to the second diamond (◇J – ◇A), a third round clears the suit. If someone shows out West turns to the spades.

36   ◇ 4 – ◇ 5   Marks: 5
           ◇ A   Marks: –5

If diamonds split 3-3, or if South started with ◇Kx, all's well. If not, West will need the club finesse. Should he, however, play the ◇A, then the ◇4, he may go down, even though the club finesse would have succeeded. To make the best of both worlds, West should lead the ◇4 away from the ◇A. That way he will know how the diamonds are before tackling the clubs.

37

♠ A 3 2		♠ K 7 6 5
♡ A K Q 10 7 2		♡ J 9 8 3
◇ K 4		◇ A 10 9
♣ Q J		♣ A 10

North leads the ◇8 against 6♡. West inserts dummy's ◇9, takes South's ◇J with the ◇K and draws trumps in two rounds. Both defenders follow to the ♠A and ♠K.

    Which E/W cards should make up the next trick?

38

♠ A Q 6		♠ 8 5
♡ A K Q J 10		♡ 9 2
◇ K Q 7 3		◇ 8 5 4 2
♣ 2		♣ K 8 5 4 3

After an opening 1♠ bid by South, West becomes declarer in 4♡. North leads the ♣7. West cashes the ♠AQ, ruffs a spade, all following, and leads the ◇2, capturing South's ◇10 with the ◇K.

    Which E/W cards should make up the next (fifth) trick?

39

♠ J 10 4		♠ A Q 2
♡ A 9 6 5		♡ K J 4 2
◇ A Q 3		◇ K J 5
♣ Q J 9		♣ 10 4 2

North leads the ♣K, ♣A and ♣5 against 4♡, South following.

    Which E/W cards should make up the next (fourth) trick?

37   ◇ A – ◇ 4   Marks: 5

Either a 3-3 spade break or the club finesse will bring home the slam.
Good odds, yet West can improve on them. On the lead, South appears
to have the ◇Q, so West cashes the ◇A, plays the ◇10 and throws his
losing spade on the ◇Q. Should South return a spade, the suit may
break 3-3. But he may not have a spade, and if so, whatever he returns
will present West with his twelfth trick.

38   ◇ Q – ◇ 2   Marks: 10

An easy contract to make — but how easy to lose! West needs two
diamond tricks. Should he then play another diamond, *any* diamond?
If so, a club from North, then another, would force him, and if trumps
are 4-1, it could be fatal. The ◇K compels South to win. He can do no
harm and West will have time to set up a diamond before being forced.

39   ♠ 4 – ♠ Q   Marks: 5

If the ♠Q holds West can afford a safety play in trumps — the ♡K, then
the ♡2, inserting the ♡9, if no honour appears. If the spade finesse fails
West will need four trump tricks. The ♡5 to the ♡J wins against ♡Qxx
or ♡Qx with North and yields four tricks also if he has the bare ♡Q.

40

♠ A K Q J 7 6 4 2	♠ 8 5
♡ A K 6	♡ J 10 7
◇ A 3	◇ J 8 2
♣ None	♣ A K 8 5 2

(N / W E / S)

Sitting West, when this hand came up, was Boris Koytchou, a Tartar by birth, who has represented both France and later the United States. Over South's opening 3◇ Koytchou jumped to 6♠ and all passed.

    North led the ◇4 to the ◇8, ◇9 and ◇A. On the ♠A South discarded a diamond, whereupon Koytchou proceeded to make his contract.

    Which was Koytchou's only loser?

41

♠ J 8 5 2	♠ A K Q
♡ A K Q J 10	♡ 4 3 2
◇ Q 9	◇ A 7
♣ 10 7	♣ J 8 6 4 3

(N / W E / S)

North led the ♣K, then the ♣A against 4♡. The second time South threw a diamond. He ruffed a third club, a low one, but was over-ruffed by West, who proceeded to lay down the ♡A, then the ♡K. South threw another diamond. Too late West realised that he shouldn't have over-ruffed. Had he discarded a diamond he would have been safe. Was it too late to recover?

    What should be the last three cards in the E/W hands?

42

♠ A 7	♠ Q 5
♡ A J 10 8 5 4	♡ Q 9 7 6
◇ K J 3	◇ A 10
♣ 10 8	♣ 9 5 4 3 2

(N / W E / S)

North, the dealer, who bid 1♠, leads the ♠6 against 4♡. South covers dummy's ♠Q with the ♠K and West wins.

    Which E/W cards should make up trick two?

---

40   The ♠ 2   Marks: 10

Declarer had two losers while dummy had two winners, but how could
he get to them?

Koytchou found a way—by underleading his top trumps to throw
North in! The ♠2 was the key card. Since North's ◇4 could only be a
singleton, whatever he returned, a heart or a club, Koytchou would have
access to dummy.

---

41   W: ♠ J ◇ Q 9; E: ◇ 7 ♣ J 8   Marks: 10

West must draw all four trumps before cashing the ♠AKQ, but how
then can he get back to the ♠J? The answer is to jettison the ◇A on the
fourth heart, unblocking! In the three-card ending the ◇7 is led from
dummy and if South has the ◇K — likely enough since he has more
diamonds than North — he is put on play and West scores the last
two tricks.

---

42   ◇ 3 — ◇ 10   Marks: 10

Why didn't North lead the ♣K from ♣AK, if only to look at dummy?
Clearly he cannot have both honours. Surely then he needs the ♡K and
◇Q for the barest opening. West finesses the ◇10, cashes the ◇A and
returns to the ♡A to discard dummy's spade loser on the ◇K.

That's how this hand was played by world champion Billy Eisenberg,
recorded by Mike Lawrence in *How to Read Your Opponents' Cards*.

43

♠ A 4 2
♡ 6
◇ 4 3 2
♣ Q 10 9 7 6 3

♠ K
♡ K 5
◇ A K J 8
♣ A K 8 5 4 2

Playing *canapé* (the shorter suit before the longer), East opened 1◇, South vulnerable, bid 1♠ and West found himself eventually in 6♣. North, whose hand was: ♠987 ♡A98742 ◇1076 ♣J, led the ♠9.

How many tricks should West make?

44

♠ A Q 9 2
♡ A K Q J 10
◇ A K
♣ Q 4

♠ 10 8 7
♡ 9 4
◇ 8 5 3
♣ A K 10 9 8

North leads the ◇J against 6♡. Trumps break 3-3. It's a pretty good contract.

Which E/W cards should make up trick five to make it prettier still?

45

♠ 9 4 3 2
♡ A K
◇ A Q 10 2
♣ A K 4

♠ A J
♡ 6 4 3 2
◇ J 9 8 7
♣ Q J 9

North leads the ♠6 against 3NT. How many tricks should West make if:
  (a) South has the ♠K and North five spades and the ◇K?
  (b) North has five spades to the ♠KQ and South the ◇K?

---

43   Eleven   Marks: 10

All the kibitzers made twelve tricks, but West was Adam Meredith, one
of the world's great players, and he naturally assumed that South
didn't make a vulnerable overcall without an ace or a king. So, to make
'certain' of his contract, he discarded dummy's ♡5 on his ♠A, ruffed a
spade and exited with the ♡K to the ♡A, which South, of course,
should have had. No expert would make this contract.

---

44   ♣4 − ♣10   Marks: 10

If the finesse fails, all's well, for West can park three spades on three
clubs. If it succeeds he runs the ♠10. Should it lose to the ♠J West will
later overtake the ♣Q, cash the ♣K and, unless the ♣J comes down,
finesse again in spades. The contract succeeds if: the club finesse fails;
the ♣J comes down; or if South has either the ♠J or ♠K or both.

---

45   (a) & (b) Nine   Marks: 5

North would not have led the 6 from a suit headed by KQ10. So South
must have one of the honours.

If North has four spades, the suit isn't dangerous. If he has five,
going up with the ♠A will block the suit. Playing the ♠J would be a
blackeye-to-nothing gambit. In (a) West would get a black eye. In (b) he
wouldn't − but he would deserve one.

46	♠ None		♠ K J 2
	♡ K Q J 10 9 8		♡ A 4 2
	◇ K Q 8 7 6 5		◇ A 2
	♣ Q		♣ A J 9 5 4

After a 3♠ opening by North, West becomes declarer in 6♡. North leads a trump, South following.

Which E/W cards should make up the next two tricks?

47	♠ K 8		♠ 10 5 3 2
	♡ K 5		♡ A 9
	◇ K J 8 7 3 2		◇ A 9 5 4
	♣ A K 5		♣ 6 4 2

South	West	North	East
1♠	3◇	Pass	3♠
Pass	3NT	Pass	Pass
Pass			

North led the ♠J, South encouraging with the ♠7. West won and proceeded to go down in what should have been an unbeatable contract.

Where did he go wrong?

48	♠ A 4		♠ K 7
	♡ A 8		♡ K 6 5
	◇ Q 6 5 4 3		◇ K J 2
	♣ J 10 7 5		♣ A Q 9 8 2

After a 1♠ opening by South, West becomes declarer in 3NT. North leads the ♠9.

Which E/W cards should make up trick two?

46 $\diamond 5 - \diamond A; \diamond 2 - \diamond 6$ Marks: 10

What can go wrong? Only a 5-0 diamond break could be troublesome. *Ceteris paribus* that's not a big risk, but after a pre-emptive bid *ceteris* isn't always *paribus* and North might well have a void. So West leads towards dummy. It wouldn't help North to ruff and — if he has no diamond — he discards. Next a diamond is ducked. A third one will be ruffed with dummy's $\heartsuit A$.

47   Trick one   Marks: 5

West needed five tricks in diamonds, and no matter how they split, South could always be kept out. Not so North if he had $\diamond Q106$. Since a second spade from him would be fatal, he should have been allowed to hold the first trick. South could go on to score the $\spadesuit AQ$, dropping the $\spadesuit K$ in the process, but the $\spadesuit 10$ in dummy would stop the rest of the suit and the contract would be safe.

48 $\diamond 2 - \diamond Q$ Marks: 10

If South goes up with the $\diamond A$, which he must surely have for his opening bid, West will score four tricks in diamonds, all he needs. If South plays low, West gives up a club. One diamond and four clubs will suffice. Note that the $\diamond K$ (J) would be bad play. South could have the bare $\diamond A$. The first trick must, therefore, be won in dummy.

49	♠ None		♠ A 10 9 8 6 2
	♡ K J 10 8 7	**N**	♡ A Q 9 6 5 4
	◇ K J 4	**W E**	◇ None
	♣ J 8 5 3 2	**S**	♣ A

South	West	North	East
			1♠
2NT	3♡	Pass	6♡
Pass	Pass	Pass	

This is a goulash, popular in Paris, where this hand came up. The cards are dealt three or four or five at a time, so freak distributions abound. South's 2NT is the 'Unusual' variety, showing a two-suiter in the minors. North leads the ◇2.

Which E/W cards should make up the vital trick?

50	♠ A K 6		♠ Q J 10
	♡ A 10 3 2	**N**	♡ K 5
	◇ A K 6 4	**W E**	◇ Q 5 3
	♣ 8 2	**S**	♣ A K Q J 5

North leads the ♠9 against 7NT.

Which should be the last five cards in the E/W hands?

51	♠ A K 2		♠ 6 4 3
	♡ K Q 2	**N**	♡ A 7 6 3
	◇ A 8 5 4	**W E**	◇ K Q 2
	♣ A K 7	**S**	♣ Q 4 2

North leads the ♣J against 6NT.

Which E/W cards should make up trick two?

49   ♣ A − ◊ 4 at trick one   Marks: 10

North's lead is the key. He wouldn't have chosen a three- or four-card suit if he had a singleton or even a doubleton. Clearly he has no club and given the chance will ruff one. West has enough tricks on a cross-ruff, so long as no trump is played. If South has one (unlikely) the ◊K will be West's twelfth trick.

50   W: ♡ 10 3 ◊ 6 ♣ 8 2; E: ♣ A K Q J 5   Marks: 10

The only danger is a 5-1 club break, so West gives himself the extra chance that the defender with the five clubs also has either long diamonds − if they are not 3-3 − or the ♡QJ. The correct technique is not to touch the clubs until the end. It's a case of 'Tails I win, heads I don't lose', always a good approach.

51   ♠ 2 − ♠ 3   Marks: 10

West's twelfth trick will materialise if either red suite breaks 3-3, and also if either defender is long in both—but only if west *rectifies the count*, concedes a trick first. Try it. Give North or South: ♠xx ♡J109x ◊J109x ♣xxx. After three clubs come *three* spades. The third one squeezes him. The second wouldn't. Hence the need to give up a trick first, before cashing the clubs. It removes an idle card, which would otherwise be available for a discard to the victim of a squeeze.

First Interval

Having passed the halfway mark, we can look back, the better to see our way forward. The next fifty problems will be harder, by and large, than those that have gone before, but no different in kind, with the emphasis always on the basic skills of bridge – looking a move or two ahead, peering through the backs of opponents' cards, guarding against misfortune.

Brilliance, heady stuff, induces a glow of pride and pleasure, but like virtue it is fated all too often to be its own reward. To win it is more important not to play badly than to play well but, unlike glowing, the rewards are tangible.

The last group of quizzes introduced a new theme – squeezes. Examples 50 and 51 illustrated the basic technique. Other, more complex squeezes will follow, so perhaps a few tips to the reader may not be out of place.

These days most of us are blasé about squeezes. We've been there so often before. Time was when only experts could execute them, when S.J. Simon posed the question: how do you bring home an impossible contract against the great Mr S? The answer was: spread your hand at trick four and claim it on a double squeeze. Sooner than admit that he can't see it, Mr S will concede the claim.

No self-respecting snob today will confess that squeezes are beyond him, yet even good natural players will falter if they do not know the mechanics. In the innumerable diagrams to be found in text-books there's a time-honoured three-card ending in which no one can possibly go wrong.

Here's the matrix I introduced in *Instant Bridge* and have used ever since:

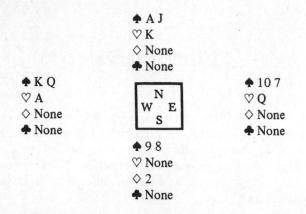

```
              ♠ A J
              ♡ K
              ◇ None
              ♣ None
  ♠ K Q                        ♠ 10 7
  ♡ A         ┌─────────┐      ♡ Q
  ◇ None      │   N     │      ◇ None
  ♣ None      │ W   E   │      ♣ None
              │   S     │
              └─────────┘
              ♠ 9 8
              ♡ None
              ◇ 2
              ♣ None
```

South leads the ◇2 and West is squeezed. Exchange the East-West cards and there's no squeeze for East discards after dummy, not before. It's a *positional* squeeze.

Now exchange the ♡K and ♠8 and East, like West, would be well and truly squeezed, unable to withstand the pressure of divided menaces, the ♠J in one hand, the ♡K in the other.

In each case the victim is outnumbered. When the menaces are divided he is up against more operational cards than he has himself, while partner is useless.

What of the first, positional squeeze? Hasn't West as many cards as dummy? No! Having to play first he has one less. Not for long, it is true, but that one moment is decisive. It may be only for a split second, but he is down to two cards while dummy still has three.

The difficulty lies not so much in grasping the squeeze mechanism as in visualising the ending, in stripping the hand mentally of the eight, nine or ten irrelevant cards. The time to do it is when you are short of one winner, just *one*, for the purpose of a squeeze is to conjure up one extra trick. True, a progressive squeeze yields two, but that's because three suits are involved and there are two distinct squeezes, each in turn producing one trick.

In the pages to come we shall add a few simple incantations to those we know already. Our spells will be more powerful and we may practise a little witchcraft, just a little, here and there, but, as before, we shall leave everything to our little grey cells, without ever resorting to black magic.

52
♠ K Q J 10 9
♡ K
◇ K 5 4
♣ A Q 3 2

♠ A 4 2
♡ A J 10 9 8
◇ 6 3
♣ 9 5 4

North leads a trump against 4♠. All follow to a second round of trumps.

Which E/W cards should make up trick three?

53
♠ K Q J
♡ Q 3
◇ A K Q J 10
♣ 7 6 4

♠ 7 5
♡ A 8 6 5 2
◇ 6 3
♣ A K Q 2

North leads the ♣A, then the ♠10 against 6◇. All follow to the ◇A.
Which E/W cards should make up the next trick?

54
♠ K Q J 10 3 2
♡ 8 6
◇ 6 2
♣ A K Q

♠ 9 8 7 4
♡ K 7 4
◇ K J 3
♣ J 10 8

After three passes West bids 1♠ and jumps to 4♠ over East's raise to 2♠. North leads the ♠A, then the ◇4.

Which card should declarer play from dummy?

♡ K — ♡ A   Marks: 5

West will then run the ♡J unless South covers. Whatever North returns West will cross to the ♠A, extracting the last enemy trump, and cash three hearts — ten tricks in all with: five spades, four hearts and the ♣A.

 ♡ 3 — ♡ A   Marks: 10

The contract appears to depend on a 3-3 club break, but it becomes a certainty if the defender with the long clubs also has the ♡K, for he couldn't keep five cards in the four-card ending. North, discarding before dummy, would be squeezed automatically. South is seemingly safe for dummy would be squeezed first. So West *unblocks* by cashing the ♡A before reeling off his winners, the *Vienna Coup*. West retains the ♡Q, dummy all four clubs, and South chokes.

   A second round of trumps? Then how would West get back after cashing the ♡A?

54 ◇ J   Marks: 5

The contract is unmakeable unless North has the ♡A. He has already shown one ace. Would he have passed with three? Possible but unlikely. So West inserts dummy's ◇J, hoping that South doesn't have the ◇Q as well as the ◇A. Placing the high cards within the context of the bidding doesn't call for great skill. It should be a habit, something one does automatically.

55

♠ K Q J 10 9 8		♠ A
♡ 3 2	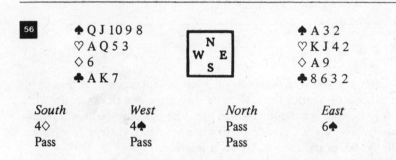	♡ K Q J 10 9 6
◇ A K		◇ 9 4 2
♣ A K 4		♣ 8 7 2

When East, who bid 1♡, then 3♡ over 2♠, responded 5◇ to Blackwood, West expected to find him with the ♡A and sailed gaily into the seemingly hopeless contract of 6♠. With luck on his side, however, he proceeded to make it. North, whose hearts were A874, led a trump.

What was, what had to be, North's hand pattern?

56

♠ Q J 10 9 8   ♠ A 3 2
♡ A Q 5 3   ♡ K J 4 2
◇ 6   ◇ A 9
♣ A K 7   ♣ 8 6 3 2

South	*West*	*North*	*East*
4◇	4♠	Pass	6♠
Pass	Pass	Pass	

North leads the ◇J to dummy's ◇A. Coming to hand with a club, West runs the ♠Q, then the ♠J. The second time South throws a diamond. West proceeds, however, to make his contract.

Which should be the E/W cards in the three-card ending?

57

♠ Q 10 3 2   ♠ A 7 5
♡ A 5 3   ♡ K 4 2
◇ A K Q J 10   ◇ 9
♣ 3   ♣ A K 7 6 5 2

North leads the ♡Q against 6◇.

Which E/W cards should make up trick two?

---

55   4-4-3-2   Marks: 10

West had one slender chance — to strip the defender with the ♡A of the minors, then throw him in. So West came to hand with the ◇A, drew trumps, cashed the ◇K and led a heart. North, needless to say, held off, whereupon West ruffed a diamond — the key — cashed the ♣AK and exited with his second heart. North had to return another and the losing club disappeared.

---

56   W: ♠ 10 9 ♣ 7;E: A ♣ 8 6   Marks: 10

To catch the ♠K West eliminates the red suits, reducing his trumps in the process to North's level. Next he cashes the ♣A (K) and exits with a club, hoping that South wins and that he has only diamonds left — West ruffs — his last two cards are trumps — and whether North rises with the ♠K or under-ruffs, his ♠K is *smothered*.

For this rare manoeuvre to succeed North must follow all the way. Here his hand is:

  ♠K 7 6 5   ♡ 10 8 7 6   ◇ J 10   ♣9 5 4

---

57   ♣ 3 — ♣ 2 (*not* ♣ 2 — ♣ 3)   Marks: 10

The first trick must be won in hand to retain two side-entries to dummy's clubs. West will use one of them to ruff a club and go back to the other to score four club winners. Why not the ♣A, then a ruff? Because West cannot afford to ruff two clubs and they are likely to break 4-2.

58

♠ J 5		♠ 8 7 6 4
♡ A K Q 7		♡ 6 5 2
◇ 4		◇ A Q 3 2
♣ A K Q J 10 9		♣ 5 3

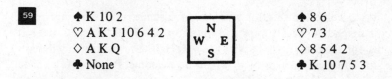

North leads out the three top spades against 5♣. On the third round South discards the ◇7. West ruffs, draws trumps, which break 3-2, and cashes the ♡AKQ. On the third round North throws the ◇8. West thereupon spreads his hand and claims.

Which card does he designate as his eleventh winner?

59

♠ K 10 2		♠ 8 6
♡ A K J 10 6 4 2		♡ 7 3
◇ A K Q		◇ 8 5 4 2
♣ None		♣ K 10 7 5 3

North leads the ◇J against 4♡.
Which E/W cards should make up trick two?

60

♠ K Q 6 3 2		♠ 8 7 4
♡ A 2		♡ 10 5
◇ A Q J 6		◇ K 8 2
♣ 7 3		♣ 9 8 5 4 2

North leads the ♠A and a second spade against 4♠, South following.
Which E/W cards should make up trick three?

---

58   ◇Q   Marks: 10

If the hand were played out West's last three cards would be ♡7 ◇4 ♣9
and dummy's ♠8 ◇AQ. On the ♣9, North, having to keep a spade,
could not retain more than one diamond. Dummy's ♠8, having served
its purpose, would now be discarded and the heat would be turned on
South. Obliged to keep the master heart, he, too, could retain only
one diamond. Whichever defender had the ◇K, it would now drop.
A double squeeze.

---

59   ♠K – ♠6   Marks: 5

If the ♡Q comes down all is well. If not, a spade ruff is the only hope.
Won't defenders lead trumps and kill the ruff? True, but you make it
harder for them by starting with the ♠K. Half the time North will have
the ♠A and a trump from him would be welcome. Playing a low spade
cannot gain. A bare ♠A is too remote a chance.

---

60   Diamonds   Marks: 5

Two club losers being unavoidable, West's only hope lies in discarding
a heart from dummy on his fourth diamond and then ruffing a heart.
For this to be possible the defender with the outstanding trump must
have four diamonds. West must chance it.

  With tricks galore, declarer guards against bad breaks. Conversely,
when a trick is missing, he looks for a lucky break to provide it.

---

61   ♠ K Q J 10   ♠ A 2
        ♡ 6 4 2   **N**   ♡ A K Q 7 5
        ◇ J 4 2   **W**   **E**   ◇ A K 6
        ♣ J 5 3   **S**   ♣ A K 7

North led the ♠9 against 7NT. After the ♠A West played the ♡A and
♡K. The second time North threw a spade. Finding adequate compensa-
tion elsewhere for the bad luck in hearts, West went on to make his
contract.

    Which were the last three E/W cards?

---

62   ♠ K J 5 3 2   ♠ 10 9 7 4
        ♡ A J 9 7   **N**   ♡ K 10
        ◇ J 10   **W**   **E**   ◇ A Q
        ♣ J 8   **S**   ♣ Q 10 9 7 5

West	North	East	South
	Pass	Pass	Pass
1♠	Pass	4♠	Pass
Pass	Pass		

North leads the ♣8 to South's ♠A. South continues with the ♠Q,
North following. A low club brings the ♣K from North who returns
a diamond.

    Which card should West play from dummy?

---

63   ♠ K Q 6   ♠ J 10 5
        ♡ A Q 8 7 6   **N**   ♡ K 10 4 3
        ◇ 6 5   **W**   **E**   ◇ 10 3 2
        ♣ A Q 2   **S**   ♣ K 10 5

South opens 1NT (12-14), West doubles and, after a rescue into 2◇ by
North, 4♡ becomes the final contract. North leads the ◇7 to South's
◇AKQ. West ruffs.

    Which E/W cards should make up the next trick?

---

61   W: ♡ 6 ◇ J ♣ J ; E: ♡ Q 7 5   Marks: 10

Before cashing the spades West played off dummy's AKs. To make up
for the 4-1 heart break he found South with both queens in the minors,
exposed to a *progressive squeeze*. Coming down to three cards he had
to part with one of the queens to retain two hearts. The knave in that
suit squeezed him again. Unblocking, playing off dummy's AKs in a
double *Vienna Coup*, was the key to success.

---

62   ◇ Q   Marks: 5

The alternative is to find the ♡Q, but there's nothing much to think
about for South can hardly have the ◇K. Consider. With ♣AK North
would have surely led a club, instead of a trump, if only to look at the
table. So South has the ♣A. He has produced the ♣AQ. With another
king he wouldn't have passed. West should take full advantage of a
lucky distribution.

---

63   ♡ 6 – ♡ K   Marks: 5

Only a 4-0 trump break presents a problem, and since South bid 1NT,
only North can have a void. So West starts with the ♡K, and should
North show out, he leads the ♡10, ready to finesse first against the ♡J,
then against the ♡9. He should set up his two tricks in spades before
drawing the fourth trump. South, marked with the ♠A, is unlikely to
have another diamond, but why take chances?

64
    ♠ 6
    ♡ 9 6 3
    ◇ A K Q J 4 2
    ♣ A 5 2

    ♠ Q 10
    ♡ A K Q 4
    ◇ 10 8
    ♣ K 8 4 3

West	North	East	South
		1NT (12-14)	2♠
6◇	Pass	Pass	Pass

North leads the ♣2, West inserts dummy's ♣9 and South's ♣K wins. The heart return is taken in dummy, then trumps are drawn in three rounds. West continues with the ♡K on which South throws a spade.
    Which E/W cards should make up the next (seventh) trick?
    Which should be the last three E/W cards?

65
    ♠ A Q 10 9 8 6
    ♡ 7 5
    ◇ 4 3 2
    ♣ A J

    ♠ K 2
    ♡ A
    ◇ A K Q J 10 5
    ♣ 9 7 6 2

North leads the ♡K against 6♠.
    Which E/W cards should make up trick two?

66
    ♠ K Q
    ♡ K 10 2
    ◇ A J 9
    ♣ A Q 10 7 5

    ♠ A 8 7 6 5 3
    ♡ A 7
    ◇ 5 2
    ♣ 6 4 2

North leads the ♡Q against 3NT. West wins in hand and leads the ♠K to which all follow.
    Which E/W cards should make up the next trick?

---

64   ♠ Q − (♠ A) − ◇ 2   Marks: 5
W: ♡ 9 ◇ 4 ♣ 2; E: ♠ 9 ♡ Q 4   Marks: 5

The ♠Q is the key play. South's ♠A having been driven out, control of the suit is transferred to North who is marked with the ♠J, as well as the long hearts. Discarding before dummy, the last trump compels him to come down to two cards. Squeezed in the majors, he must allow dummy to score both hearts or else the ♠9. A *transfer squeeze.*

---

65   ♠ 2 − ♠ 8   Marks: 10

The danger is a 4-1 trump break. West cannot afford to give up the lead, leaving dummy without a trump, while he has a heart loser. An immediate finesse parries the threat. If North wins and returns a heart, the ♠K is there to ruff it. If a club comes back, West draws trumps head on, dropping dummy's ♠K on his ♠A.

---

66   ♠ Q − ♠ A   Marks: 10

If all follow declarer concedes a spade and claims. If either defender shows out, he abandons the suit − one entry won't allow him to set it up − and turns to clubs. With two entries in dummy − ♠A and ♡A − he will play for split honours, or both with South, and will be very unlucky to go down.

---

67   ♠ K Q J 10 7 6      ♠ A 9 8 5
         ♡ Q 4 2   ♡ 10 5 3
         ◇ 2   ◇ A K 7
         ♣ 5 3 2   ♣ A Q 10

North, dealer, bids 3♡, East doubles and West becomes declarer in 4♠.
North leads the ◇9 to dummy's ◇K. Declarer draws trumps in two
rounds.
   How should he play to the next three tricks?

---

68   ♠ K Q 2      ♠ J 10 8
         ♡ K Q J   ♡ A 10 3 2
         ◇ K J 10 9 8   ◇ 2
         ♣ A K   ♣ J 10 9 8 7

North, who opened the bidding with 1♠, leads the ♠4 against 3NT.
Winning with the ♠K, West cashes the ♣AK, all following. Next come
the ♡KQ and again all follow.
   Which E/W cards should make up the next two tricks?

---

69   ♠ K 5   N   ♠ A 8 7 6
         ♡ A J 5 3   W   E   ♡ K Q 2
         ◇ A 6 5 4 3   S   ◇ 2
         ♣ A 5   ♣ K Q 4 3 2

After much scientific bidding West ends up on a Moysian 4-3 fit in 6♡.
North leads a trump.
   Which E/W cards should make up trick two?

---

67   ◇ A – ♣ 2; ◇ 7 – ♠ 7; ♡ 2 – ♡ 3   Marks: 10

The bidding and the opening lead provide the dual key to the correct play. With ♡AK North would have surely led a top honour in preference to the anaemic ◇9. So South has the ♡K or ♡A. If so, it must be bare, for North wouldn't have bid 3♡ on a five-card suit. Diamonds having been eliminated, South is thrown in with the ♡K(A) and forced to lead a club or to concede a ruff and discard. Alternatively, North's ♡A will drop South's ♡K.

---

68   ♡ J – ♡ A; ♣ J – ♠ Q   Marks: 10

Defenders cannot set up their spades without providing an entry to dummy's clubs, and if they leave the spades alone, West will have time to develop three tricks in diamonds.

---

69   ♣ 5 – ♣ 2   Marks: 10

Whatever the return, West will cash the ◇A, ruff a diamond and, coming to hand (♠K or ♣A), draw trumps. Ducking a club at trick two is an insurance against the likely 4-2 break. Needless to say, West cannot afford a second round of trumps before he has ruffed a diamond. And he must allow, of course, for a 4-2 trump break.

70

♠ K Q
♡ A K 2
◇ A K Q J 10
♣ 4 3 2

♠ 5 4 3 2
♡ 8 5
◇ 9 2
♣ A K 7 6 5

North leads the ♣6 against 5◇. South wins with the ♠A and returns the ♠J, ruffed by North. The heart return is taken by the ace. The ♡K follows, then the ♡2, ruffed with the ◇9. South throws a spade and another on the third round of trumps. A flamboyant player, West spreads his cards and claims.

Which does he designate as the last four cards in his hand and in dummy?

71

♠ A K 10 4
♡ K Q
◇ A 8 4
♣ A K Q 10

♠ Q 7 2
♡ 6 5 4
◇ K 6 5
♣ J 5 4 3

North leads the ♡A and ♡10 against 6♣. Trumps are 4-1, North having the singleton.

In what order should West play the spades?

72

♠ 7 6 5 3
♡ A Q J 10 9
◇ J 10
♣ 10 4

♠ A K J
♡ K 2
◇ A 5 4 3
♣ A 7 6 2

North leads the ◇K against 4♡. The ◇A goes up.

Which E/W cards should make up the next trick?

70   W: ◇ 10 ♣ 4 3 2; E: ♠ 5 4 ♣ A K   Marks: 10

South's 6-2-2-3 pattern being established through his discards on the red suits, his last four cards are known. Has he kept two spades and two clubs? West cashes the ♣AK, ruffs a spade and scores the ♣4 as his eleventh trick. But maybe South has kept one spade and three clubs. If so, West crosses to the ♣A and ruffs a spade, setting up the other. The ♣K provides the entry. A *trump squeeze.*

71   ♠ A – ♠ 2; ♠ 4 – ♠ Q; ♠ 7 – ♠ 10   Marks: 10

Since West cannot afford to lose a diamond, his only hope is to discard one on the fourth spade, then ruff one. That's only possible if South, with the trumps, has four spades as well. So, unless the ♠J drops, West must finesse. If that fails – or if North follows at all – the contract is unmakeable. Needless to say, West cannot afford to draw the last trump before playing spades. The same principle applies as in problem 60.

72   ♠ A – ♠ 3   Marks: 5
         Trumps   Marks: -5

With a loser in each minor declarer cannot afford to lose two spades, so defenders mustn't be given the chance to lead trumps twice. Once won't matter for West will win in hand and ruff a spade with dummy's ♡K.

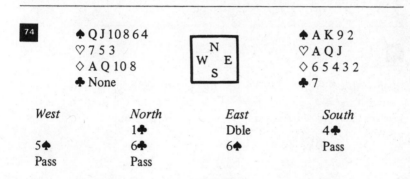

73

♠ A K Q 10 7 5 4   ♠ 6
♡ K 2   ♡ A J 7 3
◇ J   ◇ A K 7 6 4 3
♣ A K J   ♣ Q 4

North leads the ♣10 against 7♠. Winning with the ♣A, West plays the
♠A and ♠K. The second time North throws a club. West crosses to the
◇A and ruffs a diamond.
Which E/W cards should make up the next trick?

74

♠ Q J 10 8 6 4   ♠ A K 9 2
♡ 7 5 3   ♡ A Q J
◇ A Q 10 8   ◇ 6 5 4 3 2
♣ None   ♣ 7

West	North	East	South
	1♣	Dble	4♣
5♠	6♣	6♠	Pass
Pass	Pass		

North leads the ♣2 to South's ♣Q. West ruffs and draws trumps in
two rounds.
Which E/W cards should make up the next (fourth) trick?

75

♠ 2   ♠ A K 3
♡ 7 4   ♡ A 8 6 3 2
◇ K Q 10 6 5 4   ◇ A 9 2
♣ A K 8 2   ♣ 7 5

North leads the ♣J against 6◇. South's card is the ♣Q. All follow to
the ◇K.
Which E/W cards should make up the next three tricks?

---

73   ♡ 2 – ♡ J   Marks: 10

To catch the unfinessible ♠J West must reduce his trumps by three to bring them down to South's level. Then, with the ♠Q10 poised over South's ♠J9, the lead must be in dummy. That requires four entries and only three are visible, the ◇A, ♡A and ♣Q. If the ♡J holds it will be the fourth. The danger is that North, alerted by the diamond ruff, may go up with the ♡Q. Not to arouse his suspicions, the heart finesse should be taken at once.

---

74   ◇ 2 – ◇ 8   Marks: 10

Clearly the ♣2 isn't North's fourth highest. Without a doubt he has underled the ♣A, maybe the ♣AK, hoping to put South in to give him a diamond ruff. Intercepting the signal, West should take advantage of it.

---

75   ♠ 2 – ♠ K; ♣ 5 – ♣ K; ♣ 2 – ◇ A   Marks: 10

That ♣Q looks like a singleton, so West must be careful to lead a second club from dummy. It wouldn't help South to ruff a loser, so he discards. West wins and ruffs a club with the ◇A. Back in hand with a spade ruff, he ruffs his last club with the ◇9. South may over-ruff, but the defence will make no other trick.

76
♠ 6		♠ A 10
♡ A 5		♡ K 9 3
◇ K 5 4 2		◇ Q 7 6 3
♣ A J 9 8 5 4		♣ K 7 6 2

North leads the ♡Q against 5♣.

(a) Which E/W cards should make up trick two?

(b) West draws trumps in two rounds, then ruffs a spade and a heart, eliminating both suits. Which E/W cards should make up the next (eighth) trick?

77
♠ Q 10 6 5		♠ K 2
♡ A 9 2		♡ K 10 8
◇ Q J 5 2		◇ K 10 9 3
♣ A J 9 2		♣ Q 10 6 3

West	North	East	South
1◇	1♠	3◇	Pass
3NT	Pass	Pass	Pass

North leads the ♠8.

Which E/W cards should make up trick two?

78
♠ A		♠ 7 6 5 4 3 2
♡ None		♡ None
◇ 10 9 8 7 6 5 4 3		◇ A K J 2
♣ A 7 6 5		♣ 4 3 2

North led the ◇Q against 6◇. Finding the spades 3-3 West duly made twelve tricks.

Which trick did he lose?

76   (a) ♣ K − ♣ 4   Marks: 0
         ♣ 2 − ♣ A   Marks: -5
         (b) ◊ 2 − ◊ 3   Marks: 10

(a) If clubs are 3-0 South's ♣Q can be finessed; North's couldn't be since the ♣10 is missing.

(b) The danger is a 4-1 diamond break. If either honour is played first, it may fall to the defender with ◊AJ109. If low diamonds are played from both hands either (1) the defender who wins won't have another and will concede a ruff and discard, or (2) he will have to play away from his ◊A, allowing West to score both the ◊Q and ◊K.

77   ♣ Q − ♣ 2   Marks: 10

Yes, this presupposes rising with the ♠K at trick one, the key play. Winning 'cheaply' with the ♠10 could be fatal. To come to nine tricks West must give up the lead twice, so North could cash the ♠A, killing the ♠K, and drive out the ♠Q, while still retaining an entry.

78   The first (◊ Q)   Marks: 10

Whatever North led next, West would cash the ♠A and, crossing twice in trumps, ruff out the suit. A third trump entry would remain to give access to three spade winners.

79

♠ A Q J 10 9 6 5 4		♠ K 8
♡ 10	N	♡ K Q J 9
◇ J 6	W E	◇ A K 2
♣ 10 5	S	♣ A K 4 3

West	North	East	South
	3♣	Dble	Pass
4NT	Pass	5♡	Pass
6♠	Pass	7♠	Dble
Pass	Pass	7NT	Pass
Pass	Pass		

Expecting South, on his double, to ruff the opening club lead, East converted to 7NT. North led the ♣Q to dummy's ♣A. While West and East exchanged the dirty looks both so richly deserved, South pondered. 'No clubs?' asked West. 'No,' said South. Thereupon West spread his hand and claimed.

Which did he designate as his thirteenth trick?

80

♠ 4 2		♠ A Q
♡ A 8 5	N	♡ K 6 2
◇ A 10 6	W E	◇ 8 5 3
♣ A K 9 7 2	S	♣ 8 6 4 3

North leads the ♡3 against 3NT. South's ♡Q holds and a second heart comes back.

Which E/W cards should make up the next (third) trick?

81

♠ 9		♠ A J
♡ K 4 3	N	♡ 7 5 2
◇ A K Q	W E	◇ J 10 9 8 7
♣ K Q J 10 9 6	S	♣ A 5 4

West is in 5♣. North leads the ♠K to dummy's ♠A.

Which E/W cards should make up trick two?

---

79   ◇ 2   Marks: 10

The last four cards would be: W: ♠4 ♡10 ◇J6 facing E: ◇AK2 ♣4.

The ♠4 would bring North down to three cards. Having to keep a club he couldn't retain more than two diamonds. West would flick away dummy's ♣4 and it would be South's turn to squirm. Clinging on to the ♡A—North would have led it had he had it!—South, too, would be down to two diamonds.

South's injudicious double of 7♠ did not call for a club lead, but that's another story.

---

80   ♠ 2 – ♠ Q   Marks: 5

Does West need five tricks in clubs or will four suffice? The spade finesse provides the answer. If it fails, a 2-2 club break is the only hope. If it wins, West makes a safety play, inserting the ♣7 if South's card is the ♣5. If it's an honour it's covered, and should North show out, the ♣2 to the ♣8 will drive out a second honour. South's third honour will be finessed (see problem 39).

---

81   ♠ J – ◇ A (KQ)   Marks: 10

Coming in with the ♠Q, marked on his lead, North cannot lead hearts profitably, so West will have time to cash the ◇KQ, draw trumps ending in dummy and park his heart losers on the diamonds. Jettisoning a top diamond at trick two is a precaution against a 3-1 trump break. If, after two rounds of trumps, South were to ruff the third diamond it could be fatal.

60

82
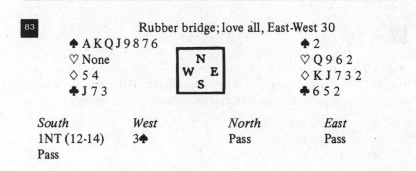

```
♠ 8 5                               ♠ A Q 2
♡ A 7                               ♡ K
◇ Q 10 9 8 3 2                      ◇ A J 7 6 4
♣ K 8 7                             ♣ Q J 10 9
```

North leads the ♡Q against 5◇.
Which E/W cards should make up trick two?

83   Rubber bridge; love all, East-West 30
```
♠ A K Q J 9 8 7 6                   ♠ 2
♡ None                             ♡ Q 9 6 2
◇ 5 4                              ◇ K J 7 3 2
♣ J 7 3                            ♣ 6 5 2
```

South	West	North	East
1NT (12-14)	3♠	Pass	Pass
Pass			

North leads the ♣10 to South's ♣Q. The ♣K and ♣A follow, North
discarding the ♡8 on the third round. A fourth club is ruffed high and
trumps are drawn in two rounds. All hinges on the diamonds. On
West's ◇5 North plays the ◇10.
Which card should be played from dummy?

84
```
♠ 6 5 3                            ♠ A J 2
♡ A K Q J 2                        ♡ 10 6 3
◇ A 2                              ◇ Q J 10 9
♣ Q 3 2                            ♣ A 10 8
```

North leads the ♣6 against 4♡. How many tricks should West make if
(a) North has ♣K976 and South the doubleton ◇K?
(b) South has the ♣K and North the ◇K?

---

82   ◇ Q, finessing   Marks: 10

The key to success lies in overtaking the ♡K so as to take the trump finesse at once. If South has the ◇K he cannot attack spades profitably and declarer will have time to set up a club. The ◇A at trick two could be fatal if North has ◇K5 ♣Axx, while South has the ♠K.

---

83   ◇ K   Marks: 5

With ♡AK North would have surely led the ♡K rather than the doubleton ♣10. So South has one of the two top hearts. With the ◇A, as well, he would have at least 16 points, too much for a weak notrump.

---

84   (a) and (b) Ten   Marks: 5
           More   Marks: -5

A poor player, finessing everything in sight, might score all thirteen tricks, but only at the risk of going down. Should South win the first trick with the ♣K and switch to a spade, it could be disastrous. Coming in with the ◇K, North would return a spade and collect two more tricks. All West need do is to rise with the ♣A, draw trumps and concede a diamond. Only declarer can lose this contract.

85

♠Q J 10 8 7
♡8 3
◇J 5 3
♣A 4 3

♠A K 6
♡K 6 5
◇A K 10 9 4 2
♣2

North leads the ♣6 against 4♠. South plays the ♣K. A pessimist, West expects the ♡A to be wrong and fears finding North with a singleton diamond and South with ◇Qxxx.

How can he guard against all these dangers?

86

♠10 9 7 6 5
♡A K J 10 8 7
◇None
♣10 2

♠K J 4 2
♡Q 9
◇K 10 3 2
♣8 6 4

North, who opened 1NT (12-14), leads the ♣K, then the ♣A against 4♡. South encourages and North continues with the ♣J, overtaken with the ♣Q by South and ruffed by West. All follow to two rounds of hearts.

Which E/W cards should make up the next trick?

87

♠K 8
♡A 9 3
◇J 10 9 8 5
♣10 5 2

♠A J 10 3
♡K 5 2
◇K Q
♣A 8 7 6

North leads the ♠4 against 3NT.
How many tricks should West make if
(a) North has the ♠Q?
(b) South has the ♠Q?

---

85   The ♣ K should be allowed to hold.   Marks: 10

Whatever South returns, West draws trumps and takes the diamond finesse. Since he still has the ♣A, South cannot put North in to lead a heart.

This is how the hand was played by Walter Avarelli of Italy's Blue Team. The distribution was as he had feared.

---

86   ◇ K − ♡ 8   Marks: 10

All hinges on the spades. Who has the ♠A? Who has the ♠Q? To find out West looks for the ◇A. If North has it − the presumption if South doesn't cover − he cannot have the ♠A, too. If South has the ◇A North is more likely to have the ♠A. Yes, North *could* have ♠AQx, but it's unlikely.

---

87   (a) and (b) Nine   Marks: 5

The position of the ♠Q is immaterial. West should go up with the ♠A at once, retaining in hand the two entries he needs to set up the diamonds and get back to cash them. If the ♠J is played at trick one and South has the ♠Q, West will lose a vital entry before he is ready to use it − and jeopardise an unbeatable contract.

88

♠ A 2   ♠ Q 6 5
♡ A K Q J 10      ♡ 5 4 3
◇ K 8 5 3   ◇ A Q 2
♣ A 6   ♣ K 7 5 2

North leads the ♣Q against 6♡. West wins with the ♣A, draws trumps in three rounds and tests the spades. South has the ♠K and returns another spade.
  Which E/W cards should make up the next two tricks?

89

♠ K 2   ♠ A Q
♡ 9 7 6 3      ♡ K Q 4
◇ A K J 9 8 7   ◇ 2
♣ J   ♣ A K 8 6 5 4 3

North leads a spade against 3NT.
  (a) Which E/W cards should make up trick one?
  (b) If both defenders follow to the ♣A and ♣K, which E/W cards should make up the next trick?

90

♠ A 10 8 4 2   ♠ K J 6 3
♡ 10 7 6      ♡ A K 3
◇ 8 7 5   ◇ A K Q 4
♣ A 6   ♣ K 5

North leads the ◇J against 6♠.
  (a) Which E/W cards make up trick two?
  (b) If a trump trick is lost, which should be the last E/W cards in the three-card ending?

---

88   ♣ K − ♣ 6; ♣ 2 − ♡ 10   Marks: 10

Now only one defender can have the master club. If the same defender
is long in diamonds, he will be squeezed in the four-card ending, when
West holds: ◇K853 and dummy ◇AQ2 ♣7. Declarer has greatly improved
his chances and it costs nothing to try.

---

89   (a) ♠ A − ♠ 2; (b) ♣ 3 − ♠ K   Marks: 10

If clubs break 3-2 dummy must retain the master spade. Otherwise
defenders will set up three or more spades before West can reach
dummy with a heart. Should clubs break 4-1 West will take the diamond finesse. Five tricks in diamonds will suffice, but the ♠K must be
retained as an entry. Hence the play at trick one, allowing West to
try the diamonds if the clubs are unkind, retaining a spade entry in
both hands.

---

90   (a) ♠ K − ♠ 2   Marks: 0
          ♠ A − ♠ 3   Marks: −5
          (b) W: ♡ 10 ◇ 8 7; E: ◇ K Q 4   Marks: 5

Starting with the ♠K will allow West to avoid a loser if South has all
four trumps, ♠Q975. If North has that holding he is bound to make
one trick. Should a trump be lost, declarer will have two chances — a
3-3 diamond break, or finding the same defender with long diamonds
and the ♡QJ. Playing off the ♡AK, the *Vienna Coup*, will expose that
defender to a squeeze.

---

91   ♠ Q 4 2
      ♡ A Q J 10 7 6 5 4   N   ♠ J 3
      ◇ None   W   E   ♡ 8 2
      ♣ K 4   S   ◇ Q 7 4 3 2
                                           ♣ A 8 5 3

North leads the ♣Q against 4♡.
Which E/W cards should make up trick two?

---

92   · Rubber bridge; North-South game and 40

      ♠ 7 6 4 3
      ♡ K J 9 7 5   N   ♠ A K Q
      ◇ 6 5 4 2   W   E   ♡ 2
      ♣ None   S   ◇ A 10 8 3
                                          ♣ J 10 9 8 7

South	*West*	*North*	*East*
2NT	Pass	Pass	3♣
Dble	3♡	Pass	Pass
Dble	Pass	Pass	Pass

North led a club. Caressing ♠J109 ♡AQ108 ◇KQJ ♣AKQ South
thought of Christmas. Nine tricks later and still to score, his thoughts
turned to Walpurgis night.
Which E/W cards made up the ninth trick?

---

93   ♠ A 7 5 4
      ♡ A 3 2   N   ♠ 10 6
      ◇ 9 8 3   W   E   ♡ J 4
      ♣ A·9 6   S   ◇ A K Q 7 4 2
                                          ♣ 7 3 2

North leads the ♡K, ♡Q and ♡10 against 3NT, South following.
Which E/W cards should make up the fourth trick?

91   ♠3 – ♠Q   Marks: 10

If South goes up with the ♠A (K) one of West's four possible losers disappears. So South plays low and North wins. If, with ♡Kx, he returns a trump, he will lose his king. If he doesn't, West will have time to ruff a spade. Should North have ♡Kxx he would have to lead trumps twice, again losing his ♡K, while if South won the second spade he wouldn't have a trump to return.

92   ♣J—♡K   Marks: 5

West ruffed the opening club and, crossing three times in spades, ruffed three more clubs. Back on the table with the ◇A he led dummy's last club. Sitting with ♠3 ♡K ◇654 over South's ♡AQ108 ◇K, he was bound to make his ♡K *en passant*. 'Next time you double, do it on your own cards,' said North reproachfully.

93   ◇9 (8) – ◇A   Marks: 5

The contract depends on bringing in all six diamonds, so a 4-0 break is the only danger. If South is the culprit there's no remedy, but if he shows out North's remaining ◇J106 can be picked up by finessing twice, so long as the ◇8 (9) doesn't block the suit. Go through the motions. North will cover the second time but not the third and West will be unable to overtake.

94
♠ A Q 2		♠ 5 4 3
♡ A K 8 7 6		♡ Q 9 5 4 3 2
◇ Q 4		◇ A 5
♣ K 6 3		♣ 7 2

West	North	East	South
1♡	2NT	4♡	Pass
Pass	Pass		

North leads the ♡10, South following. West wins in dummy and successfully finesses the ♠Q.

Which E/W cards should make up the next trick?

95
♠ A K Q J 8 6 2		♠ 10 4
♡ J		♡ Q 10
◇ J 5		◇ K 10 4 3
♣ K 10 5		♣ A 9 8 6 4

West bids 4♠ and all pass. North leads the ♣7, low from dummy and the ♣J from South. West wins and draws trumps in two rounds.

Which E/W cards should make up the next trick?

96
♠ J 9 7 6 5 2		♠ K Q 4
♡ K J 10		♡ A Q 2
◇ 10		◇ A K Q J
♣ A K 3		♣ Q 6 5

North led the ♣J against 6♠. Winning in hand, West played a spade to dummy's ♠Q on which South threw a diamond. Despite the unlucky trump break West went on to make his contract.

Which were the last three E/W cards?

♠ A – ♠ 3   Marks: 10

Tune in. North's 'unusual' 2NT shows not less than ten cards in two suits, so he can have one spade left at most. West removes it, cashes the ◇A and plays the ◇Q, expecting North to win. His return will inevitably present West with his tenth trick. North's hand: ♠J10 ♡10 ◇KJ1097 ♣AQJ84.

---

95   ♡J—♡10   Marks: 10

Cutting enemy communications reduces West's four potential losers to three. If North, winning the trick, returns a diamond, West may lose two diamonds, but no club. If he returns a club, West will play low from dummy and lose a club, no doubt, but only one diamond. Should North return another heart, West will ruff and take the club finesse in all safety. The crux of it is that North can play a club *or* a diamond through dummy, but not *both*.

---

96   W: ♠ J 9 7; E: ♠ K 4 ◇ J   Marks: 10

Leaving trumps alone, West ruffed two diamonds in hand, shortening his trumps to North's level. Next he cashed his side-suit winners, ending in dummy, and ruffed the ◇J with the ♠J. If North, left with ♠A108, over-ruffed, he would be end-played. If he didn't, the ♠K would be West's twelfth trick.

For the elimination to succeed North had to have the right pattern: 4-3-3-3.

97

♠ A J 10 8 7 5 2		♠ K Q 9
♡ K 4 2		♡ 7 5 3
◇ 6 5 2		◇ A K J 10 7
♣ None		♣ K 10

North, who opened the bidding with 1♣, leads the ◇9 against 4♠.
Trumps are drawn in two rounds.
    Which E/W cards should make up the next (fourth) trick?

98

♠ A 8		♠ 10 9
♡ A K Q 6 4		♡ 10 7 2
◇ J 10 2		◇ A K Q 9 7
♣ J 9 7		♣ K 10 2

Contract 4♡. North led the ♠5 to South's ♠K. Finding South with
♡J985, the ♣AQ over the ♣K and a doubleton diamond, West con-
ceded defeat. 'Bad luck,' said East. 'Bad play,' said the Senior Kibitzer.
    Which three tricks would the Senior Kibitzer have lost?

99

♠ Q 6 3		♠ 10 8 7
♡ Q J 10 9		♡ A 8 5 2
◇ A 9 7 2		◇ K J 4
♣ A 5		♣ K 3 2

After three passes West bids 1NT, East applies Stayman and the final
contract is 4♡. North leads the ♠K, ♠A and a third spade. South
signals with the ♠9 and ♠4, ruffs and returns a heart. Trumps are
drawn in three rounds, North having the ♡K63.
    Which E/W cards should make up the next (seventh) trick?

---

97   ♣ K – ◇ 2   Marks: 10

West must set up dummy's diamonds without losing the lead to South from whom a heart would probably be fatal. So, expecting North to have the ♣A, West throws a diamond on the ♣K. Whatever North returns, West will cash the ◇K (A) and run the ◇J, unless South covers.

---

98   Trick one (♠K); ♡J; ♣A   Marks: 5

All West had to do was to allow the ♠K to hold. Now, when South gained the lead with the ♡J, he couldn't put North in to lead a club and West would have had time to park two clubs on dummy's diamonds. Had West paused for a few seconds before playing to the first trick he would have spared himself several minutes squirming later – and that is often the way.

---

99   ◇ 2 – ◇ K   Marks: 5

The contract depends on not losing a diamond and North, who passed as dealer and has shown up already with five good spades and the ♡K, simply cannot have another queen.

If South has ◇Q10x(x) there's no hope, but if North has a double-ton (or singleton) ◇10 it can be pinned. After the ◇K, West will run the ◇J, unless South covers. If he does and the ◇10 drops, West will cross to the ♣K and finesse against the ◇8.

South *could* have a doubleton ◇Q, but that's very unlikely.

100

Game all; dealer East

```
                        ♠ None
                        ♡ A K Q 10 8 7 5 3
                        ◇ 5 4 3
                        ♣ 9 7
    ♠ A K Q J 9 7 2        ┌─────────┐        ♠ 3
    ♡ None                 │    N    │        ♡ None
    ◇ None                 │ W     E │        ◇ A K Q J 10 9 7 6
    ♣ J 10 6 4 3 2         │    S    │        ♣ A K Q 8
                           └─────────┘
                        ♠ 10 8 6 5 4
                        ♡ J 9 6 4 2
                        ◇ 8 2
                        ♣ 5
```

West	North	East	South
		2♣	Pass
3♠	5♡	7◇	7♡
7♠	Pass	Pass	Pass

North leads the ♡K.

Which E/W cards should make up the first three tricks?

100   ♠ 3 − ♠ 2; ◇ A − ◇ 4; ◇ 6 − ♠ 7   Marks: 10

West sees twenty winners, but also a possible loser, a trump, should he run into a 5-0 break. With freak distributions voids are not uncommon, so he should guard against it.

Visualising five trumps with South, he reduces his trumps to South's level, crosses to dummy and plays diamonds till South ruffs. This requires three entries and a second club may be ruffed — as indeed it would be. So West underruffs at trick one. A diamond ruff brings him down to five trumps and if, as above, the ♠A reveals a 5-0 break, he goes over to the ♣A and leads diamonds, a *grand coup*.

This high-sounding title is reserved for plays in which declarer shortens his trumps by ruffing a winner. Basically, the technique is the same in all trump coups designed to capture an unfinessible honour.

Act II

Curtain Raiser

This may be Act I to you, of course, if, being of a suspicious nature, you expect the next hundred quizzes to be easier than the last, allowing you to return a higher score and so prove me right. An unworthy suspicion, so let me repeat: if you start here you will win more marks, when you go back, over the first part of the course.

In both groups, each of a hundred problems, there are 800 marks to win and 50 to lose in penalties. These, as we have already noted, are not so much for bad play as for carelessness. We are all guilty of it at times and pay a stiff price for it, deservedly so.

Faced with a problem on paper a reader knows that there must be some point to consider. At the table, suspecting nothing, a player is all too often apt to obey an automatic reflex, to draw trumps, to hold up unthinkingly, to play lazily.

The penalty hands are not difficult. They are tests of discipline, not of technique, intended to eradicate bad habits, not to impart wisdom.

'Where foolishness is bliss 'tis folly to be wise.'

At bridge foolishness is *never* bliss.

---

101 ♠ A K Q J 10 9   N   ♠ 7 6 3 2
         ♡ 5 2   W   E   ♡ A Q 10 3
         ◇ 7 6 5   S   ◇ A K J
         ♣ 7 6   ♣ K 10

North leads the ♣Q against 4♠. Despite your proverbial bad luck you
should make this contract.
   Which will be the key play?

---

102 ♠ A K Q   N   ♠ J 10 9
         ♡ Q J 9 3   W   E   ♡ A
         ◇ 10 8 6 5   S   ◇ A Q 2
         ♣ 7 2   ♣ K Q 6 5 4 3

North leads the ♡5 against 3NT.
   Which E/W cards should make up trick two?

---

103 ♠ A K Q 8 7 6   N   ♠ J 10 9 5 3
         ♡ Q 4 2   W   E   ♡ 10 7 6 5
         ◇ K J   S   ◇ A Q
         ♣ A 10   ♣ Q J

West	North	East	South
	1♡	Pass	Pass
2♠	Pass	4♠	Pass
Pass	Pass		

North leads the ♡K, South following with the ♡3.
   (a) Which card should West play?
   (b) If North switches to a diamond, which will be West's tenth trick?

---

101   Allowing the ♣Q to hold.   Marks: 10

The worst North can do will be to switch to a heart. You will rise with the ♡A, draw trumps and throw South in with the ♣K. Whatever he returns will present you with your tenth trick. Should North play a second club, South can exit safely with a trump, but then you will finesse in hearts and again his return will give you the extra trick you need.

---

102   ♣ 3 – ♣ 2   Marks: 10

Should West come to hand and lead a club towards dummy's honours, South, with Axx, will hold up his ♣A, win the next trick and remain with the master club. With one entry only in dummy, West will be unable to set up and enjoy the suit. Losing the *first* club keeps communications open, allowing West to set up the suit without using up his one certain entry, the ◇A.

---

103   (a) ♡ 2   Marks: 0
           ♡ 4   Marks: –5
    (b) ♣ Q; ruff and discard or ♡ 10   Marks: 5

South's ♡3 is obviously a singleton. If West false-cards automatically with the ♡4 he will be sending out a signal poor South can't send on his own. In (b), having eliminated spades and diamonds, West exits with a heart. North scores two tricks and submits.

104	♠ 7 6 5		♠ A 2
	♡ A Q J 9		♡ 10 7 6
	◇ A Q 4 2		◇ J 10 3
	♣ 4 2		♣ A K Q 5 3

North led the ♣J against 3NT. West won and ran the ♡10, which held. The contract was defeated.

Which E/W cards made up the third trick?

105	♠ A 5 2		♠ K J
	♡ 7 5 2		♡ A K Q 6
	◇ K Q		◇ 9 5 2
	♣ A K Q 6 5		♣ J 10 9 7

Matchpoints: North, who had bid 3◇, leads the ◇A and ◇3 against 6NT. South follows once. Both defenders follow twice in hearts and in clubs. Reasoning that a finesse was even money, while it was 2-1 against a 3-3 break, West finessed the ♠J. It won. West beamed. East scowled. 'In trying for a thirteenth trick you nearly lost the twelfth,' he said.

Which *should* have been West's thirteenth trick?

106	♠ K Q 8 4		♠ A 7 6 2
	♡ 9 4		♡ A K Q J 2
	◇ A 10 7 2		◇ K 9 5
	♣ A 8 6		♣ 3

North leads the ♠J against 7♠.

Which E/W cards should make up trick two?

---

104   ♡ 7 – ♡ J   Marks: 5

Short of playing misère (nullo), there is no other way of going down,
even against the second best defence. Clearly North, who had mis-
takenly held up the ♡K, now won and switched to a spade, finding
South with five. As soon as West was certain of two heart tricks he
should have switched to diamonds. No distribution could rob him of
nine tricks.

---

105   ♠ 2   Marks: 10

North, having shown eleven cards in the other suits, couldn't have
more than two spades. In the four-card ending ♠A52 ♡7 would face
♠KJ ♡Q6.

Either hearts were 3-3, and all was well, or South, forced to guard
both majors, would have been squeezed. The spade finesse was a form
of Russian roulette. West survived, undeservedly so.

---

106   ♣ 3 – ♣ A (*not* ♣ A – ♣ 3)   Marks: 10

A frequent problem is to insure against a 4-1 trump break. Here the
danger is a 5-1 heart split, which would leave West a trick short. To
make up for it he ruffs two clubs. So, thinking ahead, he wins the first
trick in dummy, cashes the ♣A, ruffs a club and gets back with a trump
to ruff another. Returning with a diamond he draws trumps. Winning
trick one in hand would create an insoluble communications problem.

107
♠ K 7 3 2
♡ A 10
◇ K 5 2
♣ Q J 10 9

N
W   E
S

♠ A 5 4
♡ 6 5
◇ A 6
♣ A 8 6 5 4 2

North leads the ◇J against 5♣.
Which E/W cards should make up trick two?

108
♠ A K 4
♡ 6 4 2
◇ A K 5 3
♣ 5 4 2

N
W   E
S

♠ Q J 10
♡ K J
◇ 9 7 6
♣ A K J 7 3

North led the ◇Q against 3NT. A lucky lead. A heart might have spelt instant disaster. West won and promptly tackled the clubs – ♣2, ♣6 from North and dummy's ♣J, which held. Lucky again, yet West went down.
Where did he go wrong?

109
♠ J 10 9 7 6 5
♡ 2
◇ 6 4 2
♣ K 5 2

N
W   E
S

♠ A K Q
♡ A K 7
◇ A 8 7 3
♣ 9 8 6

West	North	East	South
	1NT (12-14)	Dble.	2♡
2♠	Pass	4♠	Pass
Pass	Pass		

North led the ♡Q. Prospects were poor, but playing for lucky breaks West made his contract.
Which three tricks did he lose?

107   ♠ A (K) – ♠ 2 (4)   Marks: 5

On a heart lead the contract would have depended on the trump finesse, but now West has another chance – a 3-3 spade break. If he's lucky, and it costs nothing to try, he will lay down the ♣A and discard a heart on his long spade. If the spades split 4-2 and North plays the fourth spade, West will ruff with dummy's ♣8. He will be no worse off than if he had taken the trump finesse at once.

108   Trick two (♣J)   Marks: 5

West smiled when the ♣J held and sighed a moment later when South, who had followed with the ♣8, showed out on the second round. All West had to do was to cover the ♣6 with the ♣7. Then, when South showed out, he would take the marked finesse. So long as North's clubs weren't Q1098 West could keep him out and so avoid the dreaded heart switch.

109   ♡ Q; two clubs   Marks: 5

The ♣A was probably wrong, so the only hope was to set up dummy's fourth diamond without letting in South. The ♡Q was allowed to hold. Winning the trump switch, West threw two diamonds on the ♡AK, ruffed a diamond and, returning with a trump, ruffed another. Luckily, the suit broke 3-3 and a trump remained in dummy as an entry.

110

♠ K 8 7		♠ J 10 9
♡ K 10	N	♡ A 7 2
◇ A Q J 10 6 3	W E	◇ 4 2
♣ Q 6	S	♣ J 9 4 3 2

Contract 3NT. North led the ♠4 to dummy's ♠9, South's ♠A and West's ♠7. The ♠2 came back. Though the ◇K was on the right side, West went down in a contract that he should have made.

Where did he go wrong?

---

111   Rubber bridge; game all, North–South 30, East–West 60

♠ A K 10 9 6 3		♠ 5 4 2
♡ A K Q	N	♡ 2
◇ J	W E	◇ 10 9 8 7 6
♣ Q J 10	S	♣ 7 5 4 2

West	North	East	South
	2NT	Pass	3♡
3♠	Dble	Pass	Pass
Pass			

North's hand: ♠QJ87 ♡J87 ◇AKQ ♣AK8.

North leads the ◇K, then the ♣K, ♣A and ♣8. West lays down the ♠A on which South throws the ♡3.

Which E/W cards should make up the next two tricks?

112

♠ J 10 9 8 7 6		♠ A K 2
♡ A Q 3 2	N	♡ 8
◇ A	W E	◇ 10 6 4 3 2
♣ 6 3	S	♣ 9 7 4 2

West is in 4♠. Defenders start with the three top clubs. West ruffs.

Which E/W cards should make up the next two tricks?

Trick one Marks: 10

The contract is pretty hopeless without the diamond finesse, but unless South has a doubleton ◇K, it will have to be repeated and the ♡A is dummy's only entry. West should jettison the ♠K on the ♠A at trick one, so ensuring another entry to dummy with the ♠J10.

---

111 ♡A – ♡2; ♡K – ♠4 Marks: 10

West's aim is to reduce his trumps to North's level, strip the hand and, in the three-card ending, lead the ♠10 from ♠K109, forcing North to play away from ♠Q8. Only by ruffing diamonds can he shorten his trumps and only by ruffing master hearts can he reach dummy to do it.

 ♡A – ♡8; ♡2 – ♠2 Marks: 0
Trumps Marks: –5

West can see ten tricks — five trumps, the two red aces and three heart ruffs in dummy. The ◇A and a diamond ruff provide the entries. Even one round of trumps — an automatic reflex — could be suicidal. Declarer would now need the heart finesse and might go two down in a cold contract. It's just a case of cashing ten winners before killing one of them.

113
♠ A Q 10 8 7 6 5 3
♡ J 3 2
◇ A
♣ 5

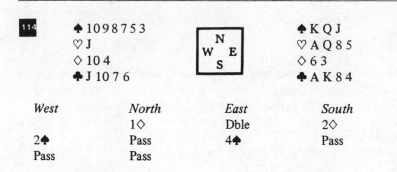

♠ J 9
♡ K 4
◇ J 10 8 7 6
♣ A 7 6 4

North leads a diamond against 4♠.
Which E/W cards should make up the next two tricks?

114
♠ 10 9 8 7 5 3
♡ J
◇ 10 4
♣ J 10 7 6

| N |
| W E |
| S |

♠ K Q J
♡ A Q 8 5
◇ 6 3
♣ A K 8 4

West	*North*	*East*	*South*
	1◇	Dble	2◇
2♠	Pass	4♠	Pass
Pass	Pass		

On the lead of the ◇K, South played the ◇Q and North switched to the ♣Q. West won and duly made his contract.
Which three tricks did he lose?

115
♠ K J 10
♡ Q J 4
◇ A J 6
♣ K Q J 3

| N |
| W E |
| S |

♠ Q 9 4
♡ A 9 6
◇ K 10 4
♣ 10 7 6 2

North led the ♡5 against 3NT, South covering dummy's ♡9 with the ♡10. Careful play would have ensured the contract. West, however, slipped up.
Where?

---

113   ♣ 5 — ♣ A; ♡ 4 — ♡ J   Marks: 10

If South goes up with the ♡Q West will lose only two hearts. If North wins and leads a trump, maybe from ♠K42, he won't be able to do it again, so West will have time to ruff a heart. Alternatively, North will lose his ♠K.

This perfect safety play has been attributed to Giorgio Belladonna — who disclaims all responsibility!

---

114   ◇ K, ♡ K, ♠ A   Marks: 10

The writing was on the wall. North would come in with the ♠A, give South the lead with the ◇J and ruff the club return. West countered by leading the ♡A, then the ♡Q on which he threw his second diamond, thereby snipping North-South communications. Hence the term 'Scissors Coup'.

North was only *likely* to have the ♡K, but South was *certain* to have the ◇J.

---

115   ♡ Q (J) at trick one   Marks: 5

South's ♡10 should be allowed to hold. So long as North didn't have both black aces West was safe. Winning the heart continuation, he would drive out one of the aces, then the other. If South had three hearts, the suit wasn't dangerous. If he had two, he wouldn't have one to play when he came in with his ace. By winning the first trick West left South with a heart to return, setting up North's suit while he still had an ace.

116	♠ None		♠ K Q J 4
	♡ A Q 2	N	♡ 10 9 8
	◇ A K Q 7 4 2	W E	◇ J 9
	♣ A K Q 5	S	♣ 6 4 3 2

Contract 6NT. North leads the ♣J to West's ♣A.
(a) Which E/W cards should make up trick two?
(b) If declarer takes a finesse, which E/W cards will make up that trick?

117	♠ Q J		♠ 7 5 4
	♡ K 9 6 5	N	♡ A J 4 2
	◇ 10 9 4	W E	◇ A Q J
	♣ K Q J 10	S	♣ 9 8 7

West	North	East	South
	Pass	Pass	Pass
1NT	Pass	2♣	Pass
2♡	Pass	4♡	Pass
Pass	Pass		

North leads the ♠K, ♠A and ♣9, South contributing the ♠10, ♠8 and ◇8. West ruffs and lays down the ♡K to which both defenders follow.
Which E/W cards should make up the next trick?

118	♠ 5		♠ A Q J 3 2
	♡ 4 3	N	♡ A Q J 8
	◇ A K Q 4	W E	◇ 7 6
	♣ Q J 10 9 8 7	S	♣ 6 5

West is in 3NT. North leads the ♡2. How many tricks should West make if both kings in the majors are:
(a) right? (b) wrong?

---

116   (a) ♣ K (Q) – ♣ 3   Marks: 5
        (b) ◊ 2 – ◊ 9   Marks: 5

Needing one spade trick for his contract West requires two entries in dummy. The ◊J is one. The ♣6 will be the other — if the suit breaks 3-2. So West tests the clubs first. Should they be divided 4-1, the only hope of a second entry will be in diamonds. So West must finesse manfully. The heart finesse wouldn't suffice.

117   ♡ 5 – ♡ A   Marks: 10

A club loser being inevitable, the contract cannot be made unless the diamond finesse succeeds. So North must be credited with the ◊K. He has shown up with six spades headed by the AK and had already, therefore, a maximum pass. He cannot have the ♡Q, too, so West's only hope is a doubleton ♡Q with South.

118   ◊ J at trick one   Marks: 5
                                      Marks: 5

Should West, unthinkingly, take the heart finesse he can go down. Coming in with the ♡K, South will return a diamond, and before West can clear the clubs, a second diamond will remove his last entry. By going up with the ♡A and playing a club at once, declarer keeps a move ahead of the defense and ensures his contract. But now, of course, he can neither set up a second trick in hearts nor risk the spade finesse.

119   ♠ A J 10 8 7   ♠ 6 5 4 3
          ♡ K 6   N   ♡ A Q 5 2
          ◊ J 10   W   E   ◊ 7 6 3
          ♣ K Q J   S   ♣ A 5

West	North	East	South
1♠	Pass	3♠	Pass
4♠	Dble.	Pass	Pass
Pass			

North leads the three top diamonds. West ruffs.
Which E/W cards should make up the next three tricks?

---

120   ♠ K Q 6   ♠ 7 4 3 2
          ♡ 4 2   N   ♡ A K 5 3
          ◊ Q 7 5 2   W   E   ◊ A K J 8
          ♣ K Q J 2   S   ♣ 3

Over East's 1♡ West bids a direct 3NT (2NT raised to 3NT in the US).
South doubles and North leads the ♡7. A hold-up would be pointless,
so West goes up with dummy's ♡A and leads the ♣3. The ♣K wins.

Assuming that declarer remains on play, which E/W cards should
make up the next two tricks?

---

121   ♠ K Q J 10   ♠ A 8 7 3
          ♡ K Q 8 7   N   ♡ A 10 3 2
          ◊ K 6   W   E   ◊ A 7 2
          ♣ A Q 2   S   ♣ K J

North, who opened the bidding bravely with 3◊, leads the ◊Q against
7NT. South follows.
Which should be the last five cards in the E/W hands?

---

119   ♡ K – ♡ 2; ♡ 6 – ♡ A; ♡ 2 – ♠ 7   Marks: 10

North's injudicious double dictates the play. West couldn't cope with a
4-0 trump break, but ♠KQx, sitting over him, needn't prove fatal.
Forewarned is forearmed. The heart ruff reduces West's trumps to
North's level. Next comes the clubs, and if North follows, it's all over.
West's last three cards are ♠AJ10. He exits with the ♠J. North wins,
but must now lead into the ♠A10 – all because he doubled. Dick
Lederer had a saying: 'Weak players shouldn't double.' The corollary
is that it's often dangerous to double strong players. It tells them
too much.

120   ◊ 2 – ◊ K; ♠ 2 – ♠ K   Marks: 10

If South, who must be placed with both black aces on his double,
goes up with either, West has nine tricks. So both the ♣K and ♠K win.
Now West can play the ♣Q, for two tricks in clubs will suffice.

121   W: ♠10 ♡KQ87; E: ♠A ♡A1032   Marks: 10

All hinges on the hearts, so West tests the other suits first. A second
diamond will doubtless confirm that North had seven. Three rounds
in each black suit come next. Does North show out on the third club
and third spade? Then he has two hearts. Does he follow five times?
If so, he has one heart or none. West starts with the ♡A and confidently runs the ♡10. Should South cover, the ♠A will be an entry for
a finesse against the ♡9.

122

♠ K J 9 8 7 6 2
♡ None
◇ A Q 4
♣ K 6 5

♠ A Q 3
♡ K J 10 9
◇ 5 3 2
♣ 8 3 2

North leads the ♣5 against 4♠. South follows.
Which E/W cards should make up trick two?

123

♠ Q J 10 9 8
♡ 10 8 7 6
◇ 5
♣ A K 5

♠ A K
♡ A Q
◇ A 10 7 6 2
♣ 8 6 4 3

North leads the ◇K against 4♠. West goes up with dummy's ◇A.
Which E/W cards should make up trick two?

124

♠ K 8 2
♡ A J 9
◇ Q J 10 9
♣ A Q 4

♠ A 9 7 6
♡ Q 10 5
◇ A 8 5 3
♣ 7 5

West is in 3NT. North leads the ♣6 to South's ♣K, which is allowed to hold. The ♣3 comes back.
Which E/W cards should make up trick three?

122   ♡ K (J) – ♣ 5   Marks: 5

West has eight top tricks and develops two more without letting in South. Say North has both the ♡A and ♡Q. He wins trick two and plays another trump. Winning in dummy West plays a second heart honour and discards a diamond. The ♠3 remains in dummy as an entry, the ♠2 having been carefully preserved.

It is simpler still if South has one or both heart honours.

123   ♡ A – ♡ 6   Marks: 5
       ♠ A (K)   Marks: –5

West has nine top tricks. The tenth will be a heart ruff, but only if he attends to it at once. One round of trumps would be fatal. Coming in with the ♡K defenders would remove dummy's second trump, killing declarer's tenth trick.

124   ♡ J (9) – ♡ 5   Marks: 5

If the diamond finesse fails West will need two hearts and hearts must come first, the ♡K being North's only possible entry. Should West cross to the ♠A, then, and run the ♡Q? The danger is that North may return a second spade and find South with four spades and the ◇K.

The answer is to lead *away* from the ♡A at trick three. Now nothing can go wrong.

125

♠ K 6 2
♡ A Q 10 7
◇ K 6 5
♣ K 5 3

♠ 7 4 3
♡ K J 9 8 3
◇ A 7
♣ A 6 2

West	North	East	South
1♡	1♠	4♡	Pass
Pass	Pass		

North leads the ◇Q. West wins in dummy, draws trumps, finding North with three, then cashes the ◇K and ruffs a diamond, all following.
Which E/W cards should make up the next three tricks?

126

♠ J
♡ A 10 4 3 2
◇ A Q 7 6 5 4
♣ 2

♠ A 10 8 7 6
♡ K Q J
◇ K
♣ A K 10 3

North leads the ♡9 against 7♡. South throws a club.
Which should be the last four cards in the E/W hands?

127

♠ A J 10 9 8
♡ 4 3
◇ A K Q J
♣ A K

♠ Q 3 2
♡ J 6 5
◇ 10 8 6 3
♣ J 10 2

North leads the ♡K, then the ♡A against 4♠. West ruffs a third heart.
Which E/W cards should make up the next (fourth) trick?

---

125   ♣ A, ♣ K, ♠ *K*   Marks: 10

With eight cards gone, North can have only spades left and after cashing three tricks he will have to play another spade, conceding a ruff and discard. Should he put South in with his second spade, South won't have another, so he, too, after cashing a club, will have to present West with a ruff and discard.

    This is how the hand was played by Albert Morehead, one of America's leading players and writers of the *grande époque*.

---

126   W: ♡A10 ◇76; E: ♠108 ♡KQ   Marks: 10

This classical exhibition of a cross-ruff is described in *Cent Donnes Extraordinaires* by Pierre Albarran and José Le Dentu.

    French international Christiane Martin cashed the ◇K, then the ♠A and ruffed a spade. After cashing the ◇AQ and ♣AK, she ruffed a club, coming to the four-card ending shown above. Poor North had to under-ruff four times!

---

127   ♠ J − ♠ 3   Marks: 5

West must guard against a 4-1 trump break. If he lays down the ♠A first, the defender with ♠Kxxx would hold off on the next round, and if West played a third trump to the king, a fourth heart would be fatal. So West leads the ♠J away from the ♠A. If it holds he continues with the ♠10, leaving the ♠Q in dummy to look after the hearts. This way he cannot lose trump control.

---

128   ♠ K Q 3 2
      ♡ A K 7 4 3 2      ♠ A 5 4
      ◇ A 5   ♡ Q 10 5
      ♣ A   ◇ K 7 4
                                                         ♣ 10 8 6 3

North leads the ◇Q against 6♡. Winning in hand, West lays down the
♡A. North throws a club.

    Should the spades break 5-1, which will be West's only loser?

129   ♠ J 8 4 2
      ♡ A J   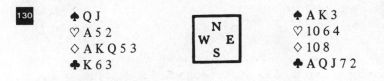   ♠ A
      ◇ 3 2   ♡ 9 5 4 2
      ♣ A K 10 6 4   ◇ A K Q J 10 6
                                                          ♣ J 3

North led the ♠5 against 6♣. West played the ♣J, covered by the ♣Q,
and finding no unpleasant surprises, duly made his contract.

    Which trick did he lose?

130   ♠ Q J
      ♡ A 5 2   ♠ A K 3
      ◇ A K Q 5 3   ♡ 10 6 4
      ♣ K 6 3   ◇ 10 8
                                                         ♣ A Q J 7 2

North leads the ♡K against 6◇. West wins and lays down the ◇AKQ.
On the third round South throws a spade.

  (a) Which E/W cards should make up the next trick?

  (b) Which should they be if West were in 5◇?

---

128   ♠ 3 — ♡ 10, over-ruffed   Marks: 5

A trump loser being inevitable, West's sole concern is not to lose a spade as well. This calls for a little care. Crossing to the ♠A, West leads a spade. If South has none it wouldn't profit him to ruff a loser, so he discards. Going over to the ◇K, West repeats the process. Again South discards. Now West ruffs his last spade with the ♡10. South can over-ruff, but he will take no other trick. Two losers have been telescoped into one.

---

129   ♣ Q (trick two)   Marks: 10

This allowed for the likely 4-2 club break. Another spade removed dummy's last trump, but coming to hand with the ♡A West drew three more rounds of trumps and could now reel off the diamonds. Simple — so long as you think of it in time.

---

130   ♣ K — ♣ 2   Marks: 5
   ♠ Q — ♠ 3   Marks: 5

In 6◇ West must discard both his heart losers and this he can only do if North has at least three clubs. So he should test clubs first, in case he has four. Then there'll be no need to touch spades at all. In 5◇ one heart discard suffices, so the slender risk of North having a singleton spade is preferable to the greater danger of his having only two clubs.

131

♠ A K 5		♠ J 10
♡ A 3 2	N	♡ 9 7 4
◇ A Q 4 3	W E	◇ K J 10 9
♣ A 4 3	S	♣ Q J 5 2

North led the ♡K, then the ♡Q against 3NT, South following high-low to signal a doubleton. The club finesse failed and the contract with it. West's only consolation was that the spade finesse was wrong, too. And yet the contract was unbeatable.

Which should have been West's four losers?

132

♠ A Q J 10 7 6		♠ K 9 8
♡ Q 10 3	N	♡ A K J
◇ A Q 8 3	W E	◇ 7 6 5 2
♣ None	S	♣ A J 8

North, who overcalled West's 1♠ with 2♣, leads the ♣K against 6♠, South following with the ♣9. Trumps split 3-1.

Where will the lead be when four cards remain? Which will they be?

133

♠ A K 3		♠ 8 7 2
♡ 6	N	♡ A 5 4 3
◇ A J 10 6 5 3 2	W E	◇ None
♣ A K	S	♣ 8 7 5 4 3 2

North led the ♠4 against 3NT and South's ♠J held the trick. In with the ♠K at trick two, West played the ◇A, then the ◇J to South's ◇Q. Another spade came back. Losing two spades and two diamonds West made his contract — undeservedly.

Which were his two errors?

---

131   Four hearts   Marks: 5

West should win the second heart, cash *three* rounds of diamonds and
exit with a heart. North can cash two more hearts, but must then lead
a spade or a club, presenting West with his ninth trick. On the last two
hearts dummy discards the ♣52 and West the ♣3 and ◊3.

---

132   Dummy: W: ◊AQ83; E: ◊76 ♣AJ   Marks: 10

North, who must surely have the ◊K, should be down to ◊Kx ♣Qx. If
so, he can be thrown in with either suit to lead the other. Seeing
what's coming, however, North may bare the ◊K or ♣Q, putting West
to a guess. He shouldn't go wrong. South's ♣9 showed an even number.
He could hardly have a doubleton club, still less, six. So he had four.
West should be able to count North's hand.

---

133   Trick one: trick four (◊J)   Marks: 5

A heart lead or heart switch would have killed the contract. Failing
to win the first trick was, therefore, black ingratitude, matched by
the thoughtless play in diamonds. If the suit breaks 3-3, the order is
immaterial, but should it split 4-2 West must give himself the chance
of a doubleton honour. The ◊2, not the ◊J, is the correct lead after
the ◊A. Evidently diamonds broke 3-3. They won't next time, so
be careful.

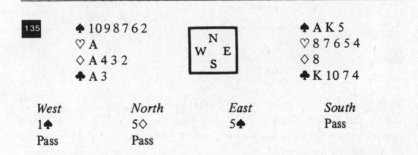

134

♠ A Q J 10 6
♡ 10 6 3
◇ A Q
♣ A K 4

♠ K 8 7 4 2
♡ A K J
◇ 8 5
♣ Q J 6

North led the ♣10 against 6♠ and West went down in a contract he should have made. Claiming that he had given himself a 75 per cent chance, he pleaded bad luck. An erudite kibitzer snorted scornfully.

Which E/W cards made up the trick on which West slipped up?

135

♠ 10 9 8 7 6 2
♡ A
◇ A 4 3 2
♣ A 3

♠ A K 5
♡ 8 7 6 5 4
◇ 8
♣ K 10 7 4

West	North	East	South
1♠	5◇	5♠	Pass
Pass	Pass		

North led the ◇K. West won and, taking no chance, proceeded to make his contract.

(a) Which E/W cards should make up trick two?

(b) Which E/W cards made up the first of the two tricks won by the defence?

136

♠ J 5 4
♡ A Q 2
◇ None
♣ A K Q J 6 4 2

♠ 10 5
♡ 8 3
◇ K Q 10 9 8 7
♣ 10 9 7

South, the dealer, bids 4♠. West calls 5♣ and all pass. North leads a trump.

Which E/W cards should make up trick two?

♡ 3 — ♡ J   Marks: 5

West played for one of the two finesses to be right, but the heart finesse was an illusion. If North had the ♡Q, the contract was safe anyway. Clubs having been eliminated he would be obliged to lead into the ◇AQ or to concede a ruff and discard. The extra chance, missed by West, was a doubleton ♡Q with South. Laying down the ♡AK couldn't lose. Finessing could — and did.

135   (a) ◇ 2 — ♠ A   Marks: 5
       (b) ◇ 4 — ♠ 5 — ♠ J   Marks: 5

West had three diamonds to look after and he had to allow for a 4-0 trump break, not so improbable after North's leap to 5◇. So he ruffed two diamonds with the ♠A and ♠K, and the third with the ♠5. Whether or not South over-ruffed, the defenders could only score two trumps. Yes, it was lucky that dummy had the ♠5 and not the ♠3 or ♠4!

136   ◇ K — ♠ 4   Marks: 10

Obviously North has no spade, so West wins with dummy's ♣9 and leads the ◇K, discarding a spade, unless South produces the ◇A. North returns another trump and again West wins in dummy — with the ♣7 if South showed out before. On the ◇10, unless covered, West throws another spade and once more North is helpless.

137
♠ K Q J 10 8
♡ A K J
◇ Q 10 2
♣ A K

♠ 7 6 4 2
♡ 7 5 3
◇ K 9 3
♣ Q J 9

North led the ♠A and ♠3 against 4♠, South discarding two clubs. West drew the other two trumps, cashed the ♣AK and proceeded to make sure of his contract.
Which E/W cards made up the next (seventh) trick?

138
♠ A Q 10 9
♡ K J 8
◇ A J 2
♣ A K J

♠ K J 8 7 6
♡ A 5 3 2
◇ None
♣ 6 5 3 2

North leads the ◇K against 6♠.
(a) Which card should be played from dummy?
(b) Trumps having been drawn in two rounds, which E/W cards should make up the next trick?

139
♠ A Q J 9 7 5
♡ A 10 2
◇ 3
♣ K 7 6

N
W   E
S

♠ K 10 8 4
♡ K 9 8 7 6
◇ A 2
♣ 4 3

World Championship at Taipei in 1971. After a highly competitive auction, in which North bid up to 5◇, France's Roger Trézel became declarer in 5♠. North led the ◇K.
Which two tricks did he lose?

137   ◊ 10 – ◊ 3   Marks: 10

What can happen? The worst is for South to win with the ◊J and return a heart. West, a move ahead, goes up with the ♡K and overtakes the ◊Q. If it loses to the ◊A, the ◊9 will give access to the ♣Q, declarer's tenth trick — before defenders can cash a heart.

138   (a) ♠ 6; (b) ♡ 2 – ♡ 8   Marks: 5
          Any other suit (or ♡ 2 – ♡ J)   Marks: -5

Let North win with the ♡9 (10). Any return will seal his fate. If it's a diamond, two clubs will be thrown from dummy. A heart into the ♡KJ will allow the ♣J to be discarded on the ♡A. Neither would it matter if South inserted the ♡9 (10) on the low heart lead from dummy at trick four. West would play the ♡J and North would be helpless as before.

139   ◊ K; ♣ A   Marks: 10

Trézel's problem was to set up the hearts without letting in South. Ducking a heart into North's hand would be the answer, but what if South had ♡QJx? Such was the case here. Trézel insured against it by allowing the ◊K to hold. The ◊A was now available for a heart discard and the suit was set up without letting in South.

     This is a variation on a classical theme, but then classical themes come up in everyday life more often than one suspects.

140

♠ None		♠ 10 9 8 7 6 2
♡ A 2		♡ 9 6 5
◇ A K 8 3 2		◇ Q 4
♣ A K Q 7 6 5		♣ 9 3

When the bidding reaches 5♣, North, holding:
♠AQJ3 ♡KQ3 ◇J10 ♣J1084, can restrain himself no longer and
doubles. His lead is the ♡K. West wins, plays the ◇2 to dummy's ◇Q
and comes back to the ◇K.
Which E/W cards should make up the next trick?

141

♠ 8 4		♠ A K 5 3
♡ Q J 10 9 6		♡ A 2
◇ 8 5 3 2		◇ A 7 4
♣ 7 3		♣ A K 5 4

North leads the ♡8 against 4♡.
Which ten tricks does West hope to make?

142

♠ A Q J 7 6 2		♠ K 10 9 8
♡ 5 4		♡ A 10 6
◇ K 4		◇ 9 2
♣ K 6 2		♣ A 7 5 3

West	North	East	South
1♠	2♡	3♠	Pass
4♠	Pass	Pass	Pass

North leads the ♡K, which holds. West takes the ♡Q with the ♡A and
draws trumps in two rounds.
Which E/W cards should make up the next three tricks?

---

140   ♡2 − ♡6   Marks: 10

A diamond ruff will clear the suit and it won't matter if North ruffs for West expects him to have a trump trick anyway. There's one danger. Suppose that after ruffing with the ♣10 North underleads his ♡Q, putting South in, and ruffs another diamond? To prevent the second, fatal ruff, West leads a heart, cutting enemy communications, the *Scissors Coup*.

---

141   All five trumps and dummy's tops   Marks: 10

On the lead South probably has the ♡K while a 3-3 diamond break is against the odds. So, with entries in plenty, West scores his trumps by ruffs: ♡A; ♣A, ♣K, club ruff; ♠K, club ruff; ♠A, spade ruff; ◇A, spade. Sitting over South's ♡K West makes his last trump *en passant*.

---

142   ♣K − ♣3; ♣2 − ♣A; ♡10 − ♣6   Marks: 5

The key is to cash the ♣AK before throwing in North. If he has another club, it may be the ♣Q and the suit may break 3-3, while if clubs are 4-2, half the time North will have a doubleton — more often, in fact, for he is known to have length in hearts.

Observe that the timing would be wrong if declarer won the first trick, as North would have a safe heart exit.

143
♠ A K 4 3 2   ♠ Q J 10
♥ None   ♥ J 7 6 3
♦ 10 9 7 6   ♦ A K Q J
♣ 8 5 4 2   ♣ A K

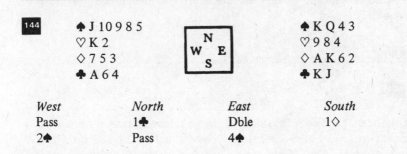

North leads the ♥K against 7♠.
 Which should be West's thirteen tricks?

144
♠ J 10 9 8 5   ♠ K Q 4 3
♥ K 2   ♥ 9 8 4
♦ 7 5 3   ♦ A K 6 2
♣ A 6 4   ♣ K J

West	North	East	South
Pass	1♣	Dble	1♦
2♠	Pass	4♠	

North leads the ♦10 to dummy's ♦K. He is in again at trick two with
the ♠A and returns another trump, South following. The club finesse
is right and West duly cashes three clubs, using a trump as the entry
to the West hand.
 Which E/W cards should make up the next trick?

145
♠ K Q 2   ♠ A 6 4
♥ K Q J 5 2   ♥ 3
♦ K J 10 8   ♦ 6 4 3
♣ 4   ♣ K Q J 10 9 8

North leads a spade against 3NT.
 Which E/W cards should make up trick two?

143   *Four heart ruffs;*
        ♠QJ10 ◇AKQJ ♣AK   Marks: 10

West has eleven tricks. With no side-entries it isn't practicable to ruff
two clubs. West can, however, engineer three more heart ruffs in his
own hand, cross and draw trumps from dummy. His entries will be:
♠Q ◇A ♣A ♣K.
   This is a *dummy reversal*. It consists of ruffing in the hand long in
trumps and drawing trumps from the hand opposite.
   Entries and the quality of the short trump holdings are the pre-
requisites.

---

144   ♡2 – ♡8   Marks: 10

One heart has been discarded on the ♣A, leaving two in dummy. Let
South win and return a diamond. The ◇A will go up and the ♡K will
put North on play, forcing him to return a heart or a club, conceding
a ruff and discard. Should South return another heart, the happy
ending will come a trick sooner.

---

145   ♡K – ♡3   Marks: 5

Doing 'what comes naturally' West would set up the clubs first, but
if he tried to cash them he would be squeezed! Three hearts and a
diamond are available for discards, but a second diamond could be
fatal. So the ninth trick must be set up before the other eight. The
defenders are powerless. As is so often the case, only declarer can break
this contract.

146
♠ Q 10 7 5 2
♡ A K 8 3
◇ 8 7
♣ 6 5

♠ A K 3
♡ 10 2
◇ 6 5 3
♣ A K Q J 10

The contract is 4♠. Defenders start with the three top diamonds. West ruffs and leads a trump to dummy's ace, all following.
 Which E/W cards should make up the next (fifth) trick?

147
♠ J 6 5
♡ A K
◇ K Q 4 2
♣ K Q 8 2

♠ 10 8
♡ 7 6 3
◇ A 8 7 6
♣ A 10 5 3

North leads the ♠4 against 3NT. South plays the ♠Q, the ♠K, and switches to the ♡J. West cashes the ◇K, then the ◇Q on which South discards the ♡2.
 Which E/W cards should make up the next (sixth) trick?

148
♠ A K J 10 3
♡ A J
◇ A Q 10
♣ 6 5 4

♠ Q 9 8 7 5
♡ 6
◇ 7 4 2
♣ A Q 3 2

North leads the ♡K against 4♠. West wins, ruffs the ♡J and draws trumps.
 Which E/W cards should make up the next trick?

146　♠ 3 − ♠ Q　　　　　　　　　　　　　　　　　Marks: 5

The automatic reflex is to play the ♠K. If North shows out, South's ♠J will be *en prise*. True, but what if North has the four spades? He will ruff the third club and there'll still be a heart to lose. The ♠Q, at trick five, takes care of any 4-1 split. Declarer plays clubs till one is ruffed. The ♠K remains as an entry to dummy and extracts the last enemy trump.

147　♡ A (K) − ♡ 6　　　　　　　　　　　　　　　Marks: 10

West needs all four clubs for his contract. How do they break? North must have six spades − since South couldn't play a third one − and also four diamonds. If he has one heart, he must have two clubs. If he follows to the ♡A he can have one club only. Now the ♣A is played first, then the ♣10, finessing against the ♣J. South covers, but the ◇A provides an entry for a marked finesse against the ♣9.

148　♣ A − ♣ 4　　　　　　　　　　　　　　　　Marks: 10

Then another club. If North takes it and returns a third club, the ♣Q will win or the suit will break 3-3. If South wins the second club he can play a diamond, but North, coming in with the ◇J (◇K), will be in the same position as before.

149

♠ A 7		♠ 8 4
♡ A K 6		♡ 8 7 5
◇ 9 5 4		◇ A K 3
♣ A K 10 8 6		♣ Q J 9 7 3

West	North	East	South
1♣	4♠	5♣	Pass
Pass	Pass		

North leads the ♠K. South's card is the ♠2. West wins and draws trumps. North follows once.
Which will be West's eleventh trick?

150

♠ K 7 5 3		♠ 9 6
♡ J 10 5 4 3 2		♡ A K Q
◇ K 3		◇ A 7 6 5 4 2
♣ K		♣ A Q

North leads the ◇J against 6♡. West wins in hand and plays a heart to dummy's ♡A, all following.
Which E/W cards should make up the next two tricks?

151

♠ 7 6 5		♠ 10 4
♡ A J 10 9		♡ K 8 7 2
◇ A 7 4		◇ K 10 3 2
♣ A Q 6		♣ K J 10

North led out the three top spades against 4♡. Ruffing in dummy, West crossed to the ♡A and ran the ♡J. South threw a spade. Despite the 4-1 trump break, West made his contract.
(a) Which were the last three E/W cards?
(b) What was South's diamond holding?

149   A ruff and discard.   Marks: 10

South's ♠2 can only be a singleton, so North has eight, i.e., nine black cards. West cashes his two AKs. If North follows all the way he is thrown in with a spade. Having no red card left he must concede a ruff and discard. If North shows out in one red suit, West exits in the other. Should North win, he is fixed as before.

  If it's South, he can cash a second winner, but must then, in turn, concede a ruff and discard.

---

150   ♣K – ♣A; ♣Q – ◇3   Marks: 10

Next, West will ruff a low diamond high, go over to the ♡K and ruff another diamond high. The ♡Q will remain as an entry to ◇A76, twelve tricks, even if diamonds are 4-1 and trumps 3-1.

---

151   (a) W: ♡109 ◇7; E: ♡K ◇102   Marks: 5
             (b) QJx   Marks: 5

West eliminated the clubs, cashed the ◇AK and continued with the ◇10, luckily finding South with both the missing honours. Perforce he led a black card and all North could do was to choose how to perish. If he over-ruffed West's ♡10, his ♡Q would be smothered by dummy's lone ♡K. If he under-ruffed, the kill would come a trick later.

  Had North the ◇J South could have saved the day by jettisoning his ◇Q. It was not to be.

Second Interval

The problems are growing harder and will grow harder still, which is as it should be for you are playing better than you did fifty problems ago — let alone 150, if you came in at Act I.

In problem 151 we came across one of the rarest coups in the game, though by no means the most difficult. The *Smother Play* or *Disappearing Trump Trick*, as it is sometimes known, has an unusual feature which it shares with the suicide squeeze. The trigger is pulled by the victim's partner. Basically, a smother play is an end-play. To kill a trump honour too well protected to be captured by finessing, the defender's hand is stripped, and when he and declarer have trumps only left, two to be precise, the victim's partner is thrown in. Declarer ruffs and the victim's honour is *smothered*. Willy-nilly, he must ruff, while dummy needn't over-ruff unless the unfinessible honour comes up.

The coup is rare because several conditions must be present for it to succeed. The technique can be learned from books, but hardly by experience, for a player may go for years, or a whole lifetime even, without ever coming across a smother play. Not so with the problems in card-reading or in guarding against bad breaks, illustrated in problems 149 and 150, or in most of those that preceded them, if it comes to that. These are the situations which come up again and again, and therefore matter most.

It is advisable to be familiar with the mechanism of the smother play, because its components — trump reduction, elimination, throw-in — are integral parts of many everyday manoeuvres. The same applies, though not always in equal measure, to other savant coups.

Learn the secrets. Savour the finesse. Admire and read about them in books, newspaper columns and magazines, but make sure when you come to the table to leave the spectacular behind you and to concentrate on the less exalted plays that bring in the money and the matchpoints — like those that follow.

152
  ♠ J 10 9   ♠ A K Q
  ♡ A 3   ♡ 8 7 2
  ◇ A Q J   ◇ 9 5 4 3 2
  ♣ A K 6 3 2   ♣ 9 4

North leads the ♡4 against 3NT. South's ♡Q is allowed to hold and the ♡5 comes back.

    Which E/W cards should make up trick three?

153
  ♠ A   ♠ J 4 2
  ♡ A 10 2   ♡ K J 4 3
  ◇ A K J   ◇ 6 5 2
  ♣ A K Q 10 8 7   ♣ J 9 2

North led the ♠K against 6♣. West laid down the ♣A, crossed to the ♣J, all following, and led the ♡3, inserting the ♡10. When it held he spread his hand and claimed all thirteen tricks.

    Which was to be the thirteenth?

154
  ♠ K 3   ♠ 7 5
  ♡ K J 4 3   ♡ 8 2
  ◇ A 3   ◇ K Q 10 6 5 4
  ♣ A 9 7 6 5   ♣ K J 4

North leads the ♠6 against 3NT. South wins with the ♠A and returns another spade.

    (a) Which E/W cards should make up trick three?

    (b) If West plays the ◇A, then the ◇3 to dummy's ◇K and a defender shows out, which E/W cards should make up the next two tricks?

152   ◇ A – ◇ 2   Marks: 5
         ♠ J – ♠ A   Marks: –5

North's ♡4 and South's ♡5 indicate a 4-4 split. It's very unlikely
that both are false-carding. Therefore, so long as West brings in the
diamonds, he should be safe. The unthinking play is to cross in spades
and finesse the ◇Q, repeating the process if the ◇Q wins. This could
be fatal. North, with ◇Kxx, may win the second time and return a
spade, killing dummy.

Is the penalty unfair? You *can* afford to cross to dummy once and
finesse in diamonds, in case South has ◇Kx. But should the finesse
succeed, you mustn't repeat it. If your intentions were pure, there's
no penalty.

---

153   ◇ J   Marks: 10

In the three-card ending the lead would be in dummy with the ♡K.
West's ◇AKJ would face ♠J ♡J ◇6. North would have to keep the ♠Q,
South the ♡Q. Neither defender could retain three diamonds.

A classic example of a double-squeeze, executed in a match by
French international José Le Dentu.

---

154   (a) ◇ 3 – ◇ K   Marks: 5
         (b) ♣ K – ♣ 5; ♣ J (♣ Q) ♣ A   Marks: 5

If the diamonds break badly the contract can still be made by scoring
five tricks in clubs. If West starts with the ♣A, however, the suit will be
blocked. Testing the diamonds first he must be in his hand, therefore, at
trick four when he will know how they break and whether or not he will
need the club finesse. After the error at trick three (b) the only hope is
to pin North's doubleton ♣10—or to drop his bare ♣Q.

---

155   ♠ A 2   ♠ 10 5 4 3
       ♡ K Q J 7 5   N   ♡ 10 9 8
       ◊ 7 5 3   W   E   ◊ A Q 4
       ♣ K 9 2   S   ♣ A J 10

West	North	East	South
1♡	1NT (12-14)	Pass	2◊
Pass	Pass	4♡	Pass

North led the ♠K to West's ♠A. Coming in with the ♡A at trick two, he cashed the ♠J and exited with a trump, South following. The contract was duly made.

Who had the ♣Q?

---

156   ♠ 7 4 2   ♠ A K J
       ♡ A 10 9 8 2   N   ♡ K 7 6 5
       ◊ K 4   W   E   ◊ A 8 3
       ♣ A Q 5   S   ♣ K J 8

North leads the ◊J against 6♡.

Which E/W cards should make up trick two?

---

157   ♠ A Q 4 2   ♠ K 5 3
       ♡ A K Q   N   ♡ 5 4 2
       ◊ 7 5 3   W   E   ◊ A Q 2
       ♣ A Q 4   S   ♣ K 7 5 2

North leads the ♡J against 6NT. West begins by taking the diamond finesse. The ◊Q wins.

Which E/W cards should make up the next trick?

---

155   South   Marks: 10

Unless the diamond finesse succeeds the contract is unmakeable. So
West places North with the ◇K. He has shown 10 points already (the
♠Q by inference). The ◇K brings it to 13. Another queen would carry
him over the top for a 12-14 no-trump.

---

156   ♠ 2 – ♠ J   Marks: 10

Until he finds out whether the spade finesse is right or wrong, declarer
won't know how to play the trumps. If it's wrong, he must hope for
a 2-2 break, or guess well should an honour come up the first time. If
the ♠J holds, West runs the ♡5, a safety play against a 4-0 split. Now he
can afford to lose a trump trick in making sure that he won't lose two.

---

157   ◇ 5 – ◇ 2   Marks: 10

With eleven top tricks West looks to clubs or spades for his twelfth.
What if both suits break badly? There's another chance. The same
defender may be long in both. If so, he would be squeezed, unable
to retain eight black cards in the seven-card ending. Playing off the
♡AKQ and ◇AQ will leave *eight* cards, so one trick must be lost first —
to *rectify the count*. Only a diamond is available.

158	♠4		♠A 10 7 6 5
	♡A K Q J 10 9	N	♡5 2
	◇K 3 2	W E	◇A 7 6 4
	♣A K 2	S	♣4 3

West	North	East	South
2♡	2♠	Dble	3♣
4♡	Pass	5◇	Pass
6♡	Pass	Pass	Pass

North led the ♠K. Fearing a ruff, West played low from dummy. South threw the ♣Q and North switched to the ♣5. West drew trumps and cashed the ♣A. When North showed out, he claimed.

Which card did he designate as his twelfth trick?

159	♠A K J 10 9 5		♠Q 8 7 6
	♡A	N	♡J 9 2
	◇J 7 6 2	W E	◇A 4 3
	♣A 9	S	♣K J 4

North leads a low heart against 6♠. South covers dummy's ♡9 with the ♡10 and West is in.

Which E/W cards should make up trick two?

160	♠10 9 5		♠K Q J
	♡A 7 5	N	♡Q J
	◇Q 9 3 2	W E	◇10 8 7
	♣K J 10	S	♣A 6 5 3 2

North leads the ♡3 against 3NT. South produces the ♡K and West wins.

Which E/W cards should make up trick two?

---

158   ◇ 2   •   Marks: 10

West's last four cards would be: ◇K32 ♣2 and dummy's ♠A10 ◇A7.
Having to keep two spades, North would be down to two diamonds.
West would now cross to the ◇A and cash the ♠A, turning the heat on
South. To keep the master club he could not retain more than one
diamond. Discarding after him, West would throw the now useless
club and score the last two tricks with the ◇K2.

---

159   ◇ 2 – ◇ A   Marks: 10

Prospects are bleak, but not hopeless. If either defender has a doubleton ◇Q or ◇K, West, having eliminated hearts and clubs, can throw
him in. If North is the culprit he's helpless. South, however, watching
the elimination and knowing what's coming, can jettison his honour
on the ◇A, leaving North with ◇Q(K)10 over the ◇J.

So declarer should play the ◇A as soon as possible, before South has
reason to suspect any hanky-panky.

---

160   ♠ 5 – ♠ K   Marks: 5

West cannot expect to make nine tricks unless he scores all five clubs.
So he must finesse the right way. An even-money chance? Only if the
suit splits 3-2. If it's 4-1 (28 per cent) West can guard against Qxxx
with South by leading low clubs *twice* from dummy and only spades
can provide safe entries. If North has ♣Qxxx there's no hope anyway.

161

♠ A Q J 9		♠ K 10 8 6
♡ A Q 9 4 3		♡ J 10
◇ A 8 6		◇ K J 10 5 4 2
♣ 2		♣ A

North led the ♣K against 6♠. West drew trumps, which broke 3-2, and cashed the ◇K. Regardless of the remaining distribution, declarer proceeded to make certain of his contract.

After the ♣A, three rounds of trumps and the ◇K, which E/W cards made up the next trick?

162

♠ 3 2		♠ A Q 5 4
♡ A K J 8		♡ Q 10 9 2
◇ A Q J 3		◇ K 2
♣ A J 2		♣ K 10 3

North led a trump against 6♡. All followed to this and to the next round of trumps, whereupon West spread his cards and claimed.

Which was to be his sole losing trick?

163

♠ Q		♠ 8 7 5 3
♡ 4 3 2		♡ A K J 5
◇ A Q J 10 9		◇ K 4
♣ A 10 4 2		♣ K Q 3

After a 3♠ opening by North, West becomes declarer in 5◇. North leads the ♠K and ♠A, South following high-low. West ruffs and draws trumps, finding North with two and South with four.

Which E/W cards should make up the next (seventh) trick?

161　◇ J — ◇ 6　　　　　　　　　　　　　　　　Marks: 10

Had the finesse failed North would have had to play a heart into the
AQ or to concede a ruff and discard. If South had shown out on the
second diamond, West would have played the ◇A and continued with
another diamond, putting North into the same unenviable position
as before.

　　Declarer was French international Jacques Stetten.

162　♠ Q — ♠ 3　　　　　　　　　　　　　　　　Marks: 10

Had the hand been played out West would have drawn the last trump
and discarded two spades from dummy on his diamonds. Next he
would have cashed the ♠A and exited with the ♠Q. Whichever defender
won, his return was bound to present West with a ruff and discard or
else find the ♣Q for him.

163　♡ 2 — ♡ J　　　　　　　　　　　　　　　　Marks: 5

If the ♡J holds or if hearts break 3-3, West is home. But the finesse
also has another purpose — to pinpoint the club position. North is
known to have six spades and two diamonds. If he has two hearts, he
must have three clubs. If he has three hearts, the third round club
finesse, no longer needed, would succeed. If North has one heart and
four clubs, West will be unlucky. Yes, North *could* be squeezed in the
black suits if declarer knew his shape in time. He wouldn't, so he
couldn't.

164

♠ K 5
♡ A J 8 5 3
◇ A J 6
♣ 8 6 2

♠ A 7 2
♡ Q 6 4 2
◇ K 5
♣ A K Q 5

North leads the ♠J against 6♡.
   Which E/W cards should make up trick two?

165

♠ A K 4
♡ J 6 4 3
◇ J 7 5
♣ J 10 8

♠ 6 5 3 2
♡ K 8 2
◇ A K Q
♣ A K Q

North leads the ◇10 against 3NT.
   Which E/W cards should make up trick two?

166

♠ None
♡ K Q 3 2
◇ A K Q J 9 7 2
♣ A K

♠ K J 8 4 3 2
♡ A 5 4
◇ 10
♣ 7 6 3

East replies 2♠ to West's 2♣ opening and the final contract of 7◇ is
doubled by South. North duly leads the ♠10 to the ♠J and ♠Q, ruffed
by West.
   (a) Which E/W cards should make up the next two tricks?
   (b) Which should be the last four cards in the E/W hands?

164   ♡3 – ♡Q   Marks: 10

A 4-0 trump break is the only danger. If North shows out, South's ♡K wins, but his ♡1097 can then be picked up. If South shows out, West ruffs a spade and cashes three clubs. Then he eliminates diamonds, and with trumps only left, throws North in, forcing a trump away from ♡K10.

This was a deal set by experts for experts in Channel 4's 'Master Bridge' series. One of the stars started with the ♡A, the other with the ♡Q from dummy! Both were wrong. North had ♡K1097.

165   ♠2 – ♠4 (or ♠A, then ♠2 – ♠4)   Marks: 10

Either a 3-3 spade break or finding the ♡K on the right side will yield West his ninth trick. The ♡K is the better bet, but West can have his cake and eat it, too, providing that he is in his own hand, in position to lead a heart, when the spade split comes to light.

166   (a) ◊2 – ◊10; ♠K – (♠A) – ◊9   Marks: 5
            (b) W: ♡KQ32; E: ♠8 ♡A54   Marks: 5

If hearts split 3-3 all is well. If not, the defender with the long hearts may also have the master spade. South would be squeezed automatically. What if it's North? South is marked with the ♠A, but North could have the ♠9. So West leads the ♠K to drive out the ♠A. If North has the ♠9 control of the suit is transferred to him and now neither defender in the four-card ending can retain four hearts and the master spade.

167

♠ A K Q J 2		♠ 10 9 8
♡ 8	N	♡ A 5 4 3 2
◇ 6 5 3	W E	◇ A K
♣ K Q 3 2	S	♣ A 5 4

North leads the ♡K against 7♠.
   Which E/W cards should make up:
   (a) trick two?
   (b) trick three?

168

♠ A K Q 3 2		♠ J 10 9 6 5 4
♡ K 10 6 3	N	♡ A Q 4
◇ A 7 6 3	W E	◇ K 10 5 2
♣ None	S	♣ None

North leads a trump against 6♠, South following. West plays the ◇A and ◇3 to dummy's ◇K on which North throws a club. All follow to the ♡AQ. On the ♡4 South plays the ♡9.
   Which card should West play?

169

♠ K 7 2		♠ A Q 6 3
♡ A Q J	N	♡ K 6 3
◇ A K J 8	W E	◇ Q 10 5
♣ J 4 3	S	♣ A K 6

North leads the ♡10 against 7NT. Testing the distribution, West plays off two more hearts and three diamonds.
   Which E/W cards should make up the next two tricks?

---

167   (a) ♡ 2 – ♠ A   Marks: 5
     (b) ♠ 2 – ♠ 10   Marks: 5

A 3-3 club break would yield the thirteenth trick, but the odds are 2-1 against it. A *dummy reversal* requires only a 3-2 trump break, 2-1 on. West must ruff four hearts in hand, then get back to draw trumps from dummy, scoring seven tricks with trumps. He needs five entries in all, so the ♠10 must be one of them. Hence the importance of retaining the ♠2 as a link and ruffing the first heart high (see problem 143).

---

168   ♡ 10   Marks: 5
     ♡ K   Marks: –5

If the ♡10 holds, the ♡K will take care of one of dummy's diamonds. If North wins, his return must perforce present declarer with a ruff and discard. A diamond will be shed from dummy. The other will be parked on the ♡K.

The right play calls for a little forethought, no more. Hence the penalty for making the wrong one.

---

169   ♣ A – ♣ 3; ♣ K – ♣ 4   Marks: 10

A 3-3 spade break (2-1 against) would yield the thirteenth trick, but there's an additional chance. If the same defender has the long spades and the ♣Q he cannot retain both in the four-card ending. So West *unblocks* in clubs, the *Vienna Coup*, and coming to hand with the ♠K he plays his fourth diamond, the *squeeze card* on which he can now throw dummy's ♣6. Go through the motions without playing off the ♣AK and observe the difference.

`170`

♠ A		♠ 8 5 4 3 2
♡ 10 5 4 3		♡ A 9
◇ K Q 10 6 3		◇ J 9 4
♣ A Q 3		♣ K J 10

North leads the ♡7 against 3NT.
    How many tricks should West make if:
    (a) North has five hearts and the ◇A?
    (b) North has five hearts and South has the ◇A?

`171`

♠ A K J 5 4 2		♠ 7 6 3
♡ A Q 5		♡ K J 7
◇ A Q 2		◇ K 10 4
♣ 7		♣ A 9 6 5

North led the ♣K against 6♠. West won and played a trump. South
showed out, but finding a favourable distribution West brought home
his contract.
    What was North's shape?

`172`

♠ A K 2		♠ 8 7 6 4
♡ A Q 2		♡ 7 5 4
◇ A J 2		◇ 10 7
♣ A J 5 4		♣ K 9 3 2

North leads the ♡3, presumably a four-card suit, against 3NT. South
plays the ♡K, holds the trick and returns another heart.
    Which E/W cards should make up the next trick?

170   (a) Nine (b) Nine   Marks: 10

From a suit headed by the KQJ North would have led the king. So
South must have an honour. If he has three hearts, North has four
only and all is well. If South has a doubleton honour going up with the
♡A at trick one will block the suit. Again all's well. Playing low from
dummy at trick one would be fatal in (a), unless South happened to
have two honours.

171   4-3-3-3   Marks: 10

West visualised the three-card ending. He would have ♠AJ5 under
North's Q109. The ♠5 would throw North in, compelling him to lead
away from ♠Q10. To bring this about West had to do two things — to
shorten his trumps to North's level, and to eliminate the red suits.
Otherwise North would have a safe exit. This could only be done if
North followed all the way, so his shape had to be as indicated. West
should have given himself an extra chance by ruffing a club at trick
two, but that's another story.

172   ♠ 2 — ♠ 4   Marks: 5

Needing four clubs West will play the ♣K, then finesse the ♣J. A lucky
3-3 spade break (35.5 per cent chance), however, would allow a safety
play to ensure three tricks if clubs are 4-1 (28 per cent) — the ♣A,
then low to the ♣K9. If North inserts the ♣10, the ♣K goes up and
the ♣J drives out the ♣Q. The first move, however, is to find out how
many clubs are needed — without paying for the information (see
problem 165).

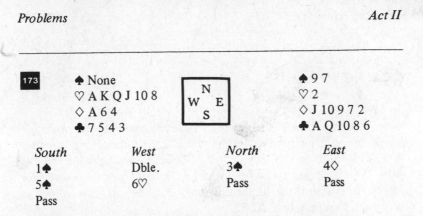

173	♠ None		♠ 9 7
	♡ A K Q J 10 8		♡ 2
	◇ A 6 4		◇ J 10 9 7 2
	♣ 7 5 4 3		♣ A Q 10 8 6

South	West	North	East
1♠	Dble.	3♠	4◇
5♠	6♡	Pass	Pass
Pass			

North leads the ♠K, South following with the ♠2. West ruffs and draws trumps in three rounds.
  (a) Which two cards should be discarded from dummy?
  (b) Which E/W cards should make up the next (fifth) trick?

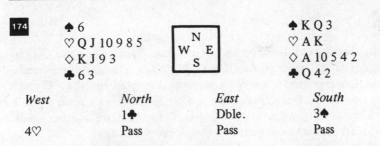

174	♠ 6		♠ K Q 3
	♡ Q J 10 9 8 5		♡ A K
	◇ K J 9 3		◇ A 10 5 4 2
	♣ 6 3		♣ Q 4 2

West	North	East	South
	1♣	Dble.	3♠
4♡	Pass	Pass	Pass

North leads the ♣K, ♣A and a third club, ruffed by South and over-ruffed by West. On the second round of trumps South throws the ♠J.
  Which E/W cards should make up the next (sixth) trick?

175	♠ K J 3		♠ A 10 2
	♡ A Q 7 5		♡ 8 6 4
	◇ A K Q		◇ 8 7 5 3
	♣ A K 8		♣ 9 7 6

West opens 2♣ and rebids 3NT over East's 2◇. North leads the ♣Q, South following with the ♣3. When West comes on play he begins by testing the diamonds. On the third round North throws the ♡2.
  Which E/W cards should make up the next trick?

---

173   ◇ 2, ◇ 7   Marks: 5
      ♣ 7 – ♣ 6   Marks: 5

South's ♠2 holds the key. Clearly he wants a switch. He cannot want a
diamond and if he has the ♣K he would expect to make it anyway.
A void in clubs is the likeliest explanation, so West should run the
♣7 – if North doesn't cover. If he does, West will need two entries for
repeat finesses and one of them must be a spade ruff. Discarding the
♠9 could, therefore, be fatal.

Note that South's bidding points to a freak distribution. A void is
no surprise.

---

174   ♠ K – ♠ 6   Marks: 10

West doesn't need a spade trick. The contract hinges on the ◇Q. To
find her West counts North's hand. He has six clubs and three hearts.
If he has two spades only, he has two diamonds and the ◇Q must
drop. If he has three spades the second round finesse against South
must succeed. In with the ♠A South returns perforce another spade.
West ruffs dummy's third spade and so locates the ◇Q.

---

175   ♣ A – ♣ 7   Marks: 10

Prospects are pleasing – so long as West won the first club, keeping the
♣8 as a throw-in card. If North has two more clubs to cash he will
then have to play into a major suit tenace. If South shows out on the
♣A West would have a problem. Now North would have four winning
clubs and on the last one West would have no convenient discard.
South, however, might be even more embarrassed.

---

176   ♠ Q 9 8 7 6   ♠ A K J 10
           ♡ K J 9 7   **N**   ♡ 5 3
           ◇ A   **W**   **E**   ◇ J 8 6 5
           ♣ A 8 3   **S**   ♣ K 4 2

The contract is 4♠. North leads the ◇2 to South's ◇10 and West's ◇A. It's rubber bridge for high stakes and the running total shows E/W to be 120 up. Making eleven tricks would earn an extra point.

Which E/W cards should make up trick two?

177   ♠ 10 8 6 4   ♠ A Q
           ♡ A 6 3 2   **N**   ♡ 9 8 4
           ◇ 2   **W**   **E**   ◇ A 7 5 4
           ♣ K Q 10 8   **S**   ♣ A J 9 7

North leads the ♣4 against 5♣.
  (a) Which E/W cards should make up trick two?
  (b) Trick three?
  (c) Trick four?

178   ♠ K Q J 10   ♠ A 8 7 3
           ♡ K Q 8 7   **N**   ♡ A 10 3 2
           ◇ K 6   **W**   **E**   ◇ A 7 2
           ♣ A Q 2   **S**   ♣ K J

North, who opened the bidding with 3◇, leads the ◇Q against 7NT, South following. West wins with the ◇K.

Which will be the last five E/W cards?

176   ♡7 – ♡3   Marks: 10

Taking even one round of trumps wouldn't be safe for West must ruff two hearts in dummy and defenders may be able to lead trumps twice more. To make the best of both worlds West should lead a low heart first, then, when he is in dummy on the first round of trumps, a second heart up to his hand. If South has the ♡A, or if the ♡J fetches North's ♡A, West will still score eleven tricks.

177   (a) ◇A – ◇2 (b) ◇4 – ♣10 (c) ♠4 – ♠Q   Marks: 5

To come to eleven tricks West will need to ruff three diamonds in his hand, so he must start at once. He will require two more entries in dummy, without touching trumps, which means that the spade finesse must succeed. If it fails and a trump comes back, he will go two down. It's a risk he must take.

178   W: ♠10 ♡KQ87; E: ♠A ♡A103 ◇2   Marks: 10

All hinges on the hearts, so West probes the distribution, suit by suit. The ◇A confirms that North had seven diamonds. Three spades and three clubs follow. How many black cards has North? Four only? Then he has two hearts. All's well. Five black cards? Then he has a singleton heart. After the ♡A, the ♡10 must win, unless South covers. If he does, West will cross to the ♠A and finesse against the ♡9.

179   ♠ 8 3   ♠ 9 7 4 2
       ♡ A J 10 6      ♡ K Q 3
       ◇ J 5 4 3   ◇ A K 2
       ♣ A K 2   ♣ J 7 5

North leads the ♠Q against 3NT. South overtakes with the ♠K and
continues with the ♠A and ♠5. After cashing a fourth spade, on which
South sheds a low club, North switches to the ◇9.
  Which should be the last four cards in the E/W hands?

180   ♠ A Q   ♠ 10 4 2
       ♡ Q 5 4   ♡ A 10 9
       ◇ A K 10 9 6 3 2   ◇ 7 4
       ♣ 8   ♣ A 7 6 4 2

When this hand came up in a match North led the ♡6 against 3NT.
North's hand was: ♠8753 ♡K876 ◇J ♣Q953.
  How many tricks should West have made?

181   ♠ A Q 2   ♠ 5 4 3
       ♡ A Q J 9 6 5 4   ♡ K 10 8 7
       ◇ A 7 5   ◇ K 2
       ♣ None   ♣ K J 9 6

North, who called 2♣ over West's 2♡, led the ◇10 against 6♡. There
were no surprises and West duly made his contract.
  Which trick did he lose?

W: ◊J5 ♣AK; E: ◊K ♣J75   Marks: 10

West hopes that the same defender has the ♣Q and ◊Q. If he has kept the ♣Qxx, the ◊Q will drop. If he has retained ◊Qx, the ♣Q will fall. If it's the former, West cashes the ◊K and returns to score the ◊J. If the latter, West cashes the ♣AK and goes over to the ◊K for the ♣J.

Though both suits are blocked, the entries provide the communications to bring about a criss-cross squeeze.

---

180   Nine   Marks: 5
          More   Marks: -5

If West plays low from dummy at trick one and South has the ♡K, a spade return could be lethal. So West wins with the ♡A. But now should South come in with a diamond, a heart back could be just as deadly. To insure against it, West ducks a diamond into North's hand. A club will be his best return, but nothing can prevent declarer from making nine tricks.

---

181   ♣K (to North's ♣A)   Marks: 10

Expecting North to have both the ♣K and ♣A, West won the first trick in dummy and ruffed a club. Crossing twice in trumps he ruffed two more. Next came the ◊A, a diamond ruff and the ♣K — the key play — on which West threw the ♣2. North could choose between leading into the ♣AQ and conceding a ruff and discard.

<table>
<tr><td>182</td><td>♠ A 10 2
♡ A 6 4
◇ K 8 3
♣ A K Q 2</td><td>N
W   E
S</td><td>♠ J 6
♡ 5 2
◇ A J 10 9 4
♣ 6 5 4 3</td></tr>
</table>

West	North	East	South
1♣	Pass	1◇	1♡
3NT	Pass	Pass	Pass

North leads the ♡9 and South wins the first two tricks with the ♡10 and ♡K. A third heart to West's ace brings the ♠4 from North. Two tricks later West claims.

Which were the tricks?

<table>
<tr><td>183</td><td>♠ A J 4
♡ A K 10 9 8 7
◇ A J 8 5
♣ None</td><td>N
W   E
S</td><td>♠ 8
♡ Q 6
◇ K Q 3 2
♣ K J 7 6 4 2</td></tr>
</table>

North, who opened the bidding with 4♠, leads the ♠K against 6♡. West wins.

Which E/W cards should make up trick two?

<table>
<tr><td>184</td><td>♠ 2
♡ K Q 10 8 5 3
◇ K Q J
♣ A K Q</td><td>N
W   E
S</td><td>♠ A 7 6 5
♡ A 2
◇ A 10 2
♣ J 4 3 2</td></tr>
</table>

North leads the ◇9 against 7♡. The trick is taken with the ◇J. All follow to the ♡K.

Which E/W cards should make up the next two tricks?

---

182   ♣A – ♣3; ♣K – ♣4   Marks: 10

So long as both defenders follow the contract is a certainty. Overtaking the ♣2 in dummy (trick seven) West runs the ◇J and, if it holds, the ◇10. Whether or not North holds up the ◇Q, West has at least three tricks in diamonds, all he needs, without letting South in.

183   ♠4 – ♡Q   Marks: 10

Were West to ruff at trick two with dummy's ♡6, South might over-ruff and return a trump, killing the contract. So West ruffs high, returns with a club ruff (safest) and trumps the ♠J with the ♡6. Let South over-ruff. The defence can score no other trick.

184   ♠2 – ♠A; ♠5 – ♡3   Marks: 10

The only danger is a 4-1 trump break. If North is the culprit there's no hope, but if it's South his ♡J can be caught. First West must reduce his trumps to the same level. Hence the spade ruff. The ♡A will reveal the position. If North shows out, another spade is ruffed. There is now trump parity. With bated breath West cashes the ♣AKQ. South follows? West overtakes the ◇K with the ◇A and plays the ♣J, followed if South doesn't ruff by the ◇10, which will apply the *coup de grace*. Note the ♡K at trick two, visualising the danger of a 4-1 trump break.

185

♠ A 5 4		♠ 8 6 3
♡ A K Q 4	N	♡ 7 5 2
◇ 9 7 3	W E	◇ A K Q 10
♣ A 9 2	S	♣ 8 5 4

North led the ♠Q against 3NT. South overtook with the ♠K, held the trick and continued with the ♠7. Though both red suits broke 4-2 and the ◇J didn't drop, West made his contract.

What was North's distribution?

186

♠ K J 4		♠ A 2
♡ K 6 4	N	♡ 9 8 7 5
◇ J 10 9 8 5	W E	◇ K Q 7
♣ 9 8	S	♣ A K Q 6

North led the ♠3 against 3NT and West went down in a contract which he should have made.

Where did he go wrong? Which E/W cards made up the fatal trick?

187

♠ A K 4		♠ 10
♡ A 10 6 5	N	♡ 9 4 2
◇ A 10 9 3	W E	◇ 6 4 2
♣ 3 2	S	♣ A K Q 10 5 4

North leads the ♠Q. West wins and leads the ♣3, covering North's ♣7 with dummy's ♣10.

What is the contract?

185   5-2-2-4   Marks: 10

West won the second spade and returned another, allowing North to cash two more. South shed clubs, but what could he then throw on the ♣A? Down to seven cards he couldn't keep eight red ones and fell victim to a *suicide squeeze*. Had North cashed one spade fewer, South could have been thrown in with the fourth heart and forced to lead a diamond. His hand: ♠ K 7 ♡ 10 9 8 6 ◊ J 8 5 4 ♣ Q 7 6.

186   ♠ 2 – ♠ K (♠ J)   Marks: 0
           Any other reply   Marks: –5

West had nine tricks whatever the distribution, but he yielded to the temptation of a 'cheap' trick in spades, playing low from dummy at trick one. The ◊A was held up and now West had no entry. Had he gone up with the ♠A nothing could have hurt him.

No reward for not committing suicide. The penalty is for gross carelessness.

187   2NT   Marks: 5

By inserting the ♣10 West makes certain of four club tricks, all he needs in 2NT. Were the contract 3NT he would require five tricks in clubs and to guard against a 5-0 break he would play low from both hands. If South showed out the marked finesse would bring in the rest of the suit.

188

♠ A Q 10 7 5 4		♠ K 8
♡ J 4 3		♡ A K Q 5 2
◇ A 10 9		◇ 5 4 3 2
♣ 2		♣ A Q

North led the ◇K against 6♠. West won and began to draw trumps. When, on the second round, South showed out, he successfully finessed the ♣Q and discarded one diamond on the ♣A and another on dummy's fourth heart, not caring whether or not North ruffed.

Was that the right play? If not, where did West go wrong?

189

♠ A K Q J 2		♠ 10 3
♡ 6 4 3 2		♡ 8 5
◇ 2		◇ A K 7 6 4 3
♣ 8 7 5		♣ A K 2

North leads the ♡K against 4♠ and switches to a trump.

Which E/W cards should make up the next trick?

190

♠ A Q J 10 6 4		♠ K 3 2
♡ None	N	♡ A K
◇ A K	W E	◇ J 10 9 8 7
♣ A Q 6 3 2	S	♣ 7 5 4

North leads the ♡5 against 6♠.

Which E/W cards should make up trick two?

No. Trick four, the club finesse   Marks: 10

Unless North has three hearts the contract is unmakeable. So West should test the hearts first. If South follows twice he will need the club finesse. But maybe South has a singleton leaving four for North. Then the club finesse will be superfluous, a black eye to nothing. West must be careful, however, to win the third heart in hand—in case he needs the finesse. This is a standard play, but easy to overlook at the table.

189   ◇ 2 – ◇ 3   Marks: 10

Whatever the return, West will draw trumps, cross to the ♣A, cash the ◇AK and ruff a diamond, if need be. The purpose in ducking on the first round of diamonds is to insure against the likely 4-2 breaks in diamonds and in trumps. Meanwhile a trump remains in dummy, so declarer can't be forced with a third round of hearts.

190   ♡ K – ◇ K   Marks: 10

West has eleven top tricks and with only one certain entry in dummy he cannot set up and enjoy a third diamond. So he jettisons the ◇AK on the ♡AK and leads the ◇J discarding a club unless South covers.
    What a lucky lead!

191   ♠ K Q J 10 8 7   ♠ 9 5
         ♡ 6 5 2   ♡ Q 9 6
         ◇ K 3   N   ◇ J 7 5
         ♣ A Q   W   E   ♣ K J 10 9 8
                      S

Contract 4♠: In response to South's opening bid of 1◇ North led the
◇2, the ◇5 from dummy, the ◇10 from South and the ◇K from West.
In with the ♠A at trick two, South laid down the ♡AK and, putting
North in with the ◇Q, ruffed the heart return. Good defence, but
far-sighted play could have circumvented it.
     How?

192   ♠ 10 8   ♠ J 3 2
         ♡ K Q 10 9 8   ♡ A 2
         ◇ K Q 4   N   ◇ A J 7 6 5
         ♣ A 6 4   W   E   ♣ 7 5 2
                      S

North leads the ♠K, ♠A and a low spade against 4♡. West ruffs.
     Which E/W cards should make up the next trick?

193   ♠ A J 2   ♠ K
         ♡ J 5 4   ♡ A 10 3 2
         ◇ A Q 3   N   ◇ J 10 9
         ♣ K Q 8 3   W   E   ♣ J 10 9 5 4
                      S

North leads the ♠10 against 3NT.
     Which E/W cards should make up trick two?

191   ◇ J at trick one   Marks: 10

South's ◇A wins — ducking wouldn't help — and North no longer has an entry. Was South running a risk by inserting the ◇10? Hardly. Had North the ◇K he would have doubtless led it, if only to look at the table, in case a switch was required.

192   ♡ 10 – ♡ 2   Marks: 10

Unless West is careful the likely 4-2 trump break will defeat the contract. If all the trumps are drawn, he will have a spade (or two) to lose. If he leaves the ♡J out, it will descend on the third round of diamonds and he will lose two clubs. Running the ♡10 is the answer. Should South win and return a spade, West will ruff in dummy and draw trumps.

193   ◇ J – ◇ Q   Marks: 10

Driving out the ♣A ensures eight tricks. A second diamond yields the ninth. Simple? Try it. A spade from South, when he is in with the ♣A, could be fatal. Run the ◇J at trick two? A heart return could be equally lethal, cutting West off from dummy's fifth club should either defender have ♣Axxx. Overtaking the ◇J leaves the ◇10 as an entry. Now, on a heart return, West can afford to play the ♡A.

194

♠ K Q J 10 3 2		♠ 9 7 5
♡ K J	N	♡ 10 9
◇ A 10	W E	◇ 9 6
♣ J 5 2	S	♣ A K Q 10 6 3

North, who opened the bidding with 1◇, led the ◇K against 4♠. It was an easy contract to make, but easier still to lose, and West fell from grace.

Which E/W cards made up the trick that cost the contract?

195

♠ K J 3 2		♠ Q 5 4
♡ A K	N	♡ 7 3 2
◇ A Q 4	W E	◇ K 10 8
♣ 10 6 4 2	S	♣ A Q J 9

South	West	North	East
1♡	1NT	Pass	3NT
Pass	Pass	Pass	

North leads the ♡9.

(a) Which E/W cards should make up trick two?

(b) If West is on play, which E/W cards should make up the third trick?

196

♠ A K 7		♠ 8 4 2
♡ K Q 9 8	N	♡ A J 10 7
◇ A 8 5 4 2	W E	◇ 9
♣ 5	S	♣ A 10 6 3 2

North leads the ♣K against 6♡. West goes up with dummy's ♣A.

Which E/W cards should make up the next trick?

194   ◊A (◊K) – ◊6 (Trick one)   Marks: 5

West won the first trick, but North came in at trick two with the ♠A and led a low diamond, seeing his only chance in finding South with the ◊J. He had it and promptly returned a heart to North's ♡AQ. Unlucky? Certainly, but there was no need to be. If North is allowed to hold the first trick, South will have no entry and West will be safe for evermore.

195   (a) ♣2 – ♣A   Marks: 5
           (b) ♠4 – ♠K   Marks: 5

South must have the ♣K and once he sets up his hearts it will be too late for West to look for a ninth trick. So, before letting South in, West leads a low spade from dummy. If South wins with the ♠A, West has nine tricks. If South plays low, West sets up two more tricks in clubs.

196   ♠2 – ♠K   Marks: 5
           Trumps   Marks: -5

West counts: ♠AK, ◊A, ♣A and eight more tricks on a complete cross-ruff in the minors. While this is in progress, however, defenders, unable to follow suit, will throw spades and in the three-card ending a spade will surely be ruffed. The ♠AK should, therefore, be cashed at once. A golden rule in cross-ruffing: first cash winners in the side-suits.

197

♠ A 7 6
♡ Q J 10 8 6
◇ 7
♣ A K J 2

♠ Q J 9
♡ 5
◇ A K Q 10 3 2
♣ 6 5 3

In a match, North led the ♠4 against 3NT. South had:
♠K10 ♡AK32 ◇J96 ♣Q1098. One West made nine tricks, the other thirteen.

Which E/W cards made up the trick on which declarer fell from grace?

198

♠ A K Q 7 6 3
♡ A K 3
◇ K J
♣ K J

♠ 4 2
♡ 8 6 5 2
◇ A 7 6
♣ A 5 4 3

North leads the ♠J against 6♠. South follows once, but on the next two rounds of trumps he throws the ♣2 and ◇2.

Which E/W cards should make up the next two tricks?

199

♠ A K
♡ K J 9 7
◇ K Q J 10 9
♣ A K

♠ 5 4 3 2
♡ 6 3
◇ A 8 7 6
♣ J 10 9

North leads the ♠Q against 5◇.

Which E/W cards should make up trick two?

197   ♠Q (♠K) – ♠A (trick one)   Marks: 5

West had a chance to recover by letting the ♠K hold, but playing dummy's ♠Q was bad. With ♠K10x South would hold off. Either way, there would be no entry to dummy's long diamonds if the suit broke 4-2, the likely division. West should leave the ♠QJ intact as a vital entry and finesse the ◇10 to guard against a 4-2 split, so ensuring nine tricks. As the cards are, playing badly, he scores ten tricks in spades and diamonds and his last winner squeezes South in hearts and clubs. The club finesse brings home four more tricks!

198   ♡A – ♡2; ♡K – ♡5   Marks: 10

Next a trump. West's best chance is to find North with a doubleton heart. He will then have to lead into a minor suit tenace, the ace in the other minor providing an entry to dummy. When a contract can't be made without a fair measure of luck, wishful thinking should be the order of the day.

199   Hearts   Marks: 5
       A trump   Marks: –5

With nine top tricks West needs two heart ruffs in dummy. He cannot afford to cross to the ◇A to lead a heart towards his honours. If trumps are 3-1 he could be left with one trump in dummy to ruff two hearts (see problem 176).

200

♠ A K 4
♡ Q
◇ A K 5 2
♣ A Q J 5 2

```
    N
 W     E
    S
```

♠ 8 6 5
♡ A K 10 9 8 7
◇ 9 3
♣ K 3

North leads the ♠Q against 6NT. West wins.
Which E/W cards should make up trick two?

200   ♡ Q – ♡ A   Marks: 5

An *embarras de richesse* is apt to make declarers careless. When this hand came up at rubber bridge, West, playing quickly and confidently, cashed the ♡Q, crossed to the ♣K and didn't worry unduly when North showed out on the third round of hearts. Not until the 5-1 club break came to light did he plead bad luck. And so it was – for his partner. With a surfeit of winners and no loser in sight, all West had to do was to overtake the ♡Q, cash the ♡K and concede a heart, leaving the ♣K as an entry.

It is with malice aforethought that I have selected this far from difficult problem to conclude the series, for it isn't the complex plays and savant coups that matter most at bridge. It is the straightforward contracts requiring a little forethought, easy to make, easier still to lose, that spell success or failure – which is where we came in.

Final Curtain

We've won. That was a foregone conclusion. The question is: by how much?

Whether you started at the beginning, or as a cynic, halfway through, I will have proved my point. Your score will be higher for the second hundred problems than for the first. Admittedly, mine is a moral victory. Yours is tangible and solid, and what's more, you have a yardstick to measure your success.

Maybe, like Monsieur Jourdain, who spoke prose all his life without knowing it, you have been executing skilful manoeuvres simply by exercising the gifts of nature, 'flair', instinct, second sight. Maybe you were already an accomplished technician, familiar with the mechanics of end-plays and squeezes, dummy reversals and scissors coups. Either way you will have played better by the time you reached quiz 100 — or 200 — than when you began. Even if you knew the theory, the practice as you went along must have sharpened the edge of your play. But that is only part of the story. There's another factor at work in the technique of winning, transcending many others in importance.

As dummy goes down and he identifies the problems it poses, the expert looks for ways of bending the odds, of giving himself extra chances. Bad breaks are inevitable. Bad luck isn't. As a pessimist the expert allows for grievous misfortune, like the 5-0 trump break in problem 51. As an optimist he is quick to exploit a favourable layout, like the distribution in problem 151.

Both examples, and many that are less striking, illustrate the same approach — the underlying assumption that no contract is as easy or as difficult as it seems, but that all are makeable.

If you can meet triumph and disaster and treat these two imposters just the same, you'll bring home many contracts that would otherwise elude you.

It was because I knew that a hundred problems would help you to cultivate this approach that I was so confident in issuing my challenge. I will now issue another. Pick up this book six months hence. Reverse the order in which you have tackled the problems this time and you will find that the same thing will happen again. You will return a higher score for the second hundred hands than for the first, but with this difference — both scores will be higher than on this, your first reading. Cards fade quickly from one's memory and it will not be because you can recall the hands, but because you will have acquired the know-how and the habit of loading the dice in your favour and of never accepting that twice two make four if, with a little judicious manipulation, the addition can be carried to five or kept down to three.